HOW TO LIVE IN THE CARIBBEAN

Sydney Hunt

CARIBBEAN

First published 1985
Reprinted 1986, 1988
Revised edition 1989

Published by *Macmillan Publishers Ltd*
London and Basingstoke
*Associated companies and representatives in Accra,
Auckland, Delhi, Dublin, Gaborone, Hamburg, Harare,
Hong Kong, Kuala Lumpur, Lagos, Manzini, Melbourne,
Mexico City, Nairobi, New York, Singapore, Tokyo*

ISBN 0—333—51015—1

Printed in Hong Kong

Acknowledgements

Large parts of this book have been ruthlessly plagiarized from *How To Retire in the British Virgins*, by S. Hunt, but with the consent of the author. The figures have come from island government sources, accurate as of December 1983.

All the photographs for the photographic section were taken by the author.

Illustrations by George Craig.

This book was originally
How to Retire to the Caribbean

But during the last ten years the Caribbean has changed.

It is no longer the rich man's playground, the retiree's dreamland. The average age of landseekers is now between forty-five and fifty-five. Even thirty year olds are strong among the new land or house or condo investors, gaining an earlier start on early retirement. An emerging population travels between home-base and their Caribbean interests, creating demand for long-term rentals.

To include this expanded market this book has been updated, enlarged in its scope to serve all ages now seeking the better life of this island world.

Contents

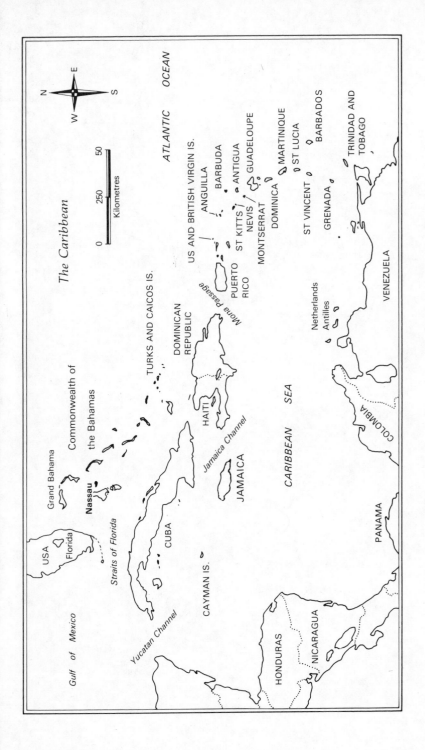

The Caribbean

ONE
Pre-plan your plan

Whether you face retirement urgently or not for years, you will be better off if you turn pre-retirement limbo into this adventure.

Almost twenty years ago I confronted my wife theatrically.

'Either we plan early retirement, or – I kill myself! You can have it all right now.'

Frances had her own experienced way of lowering the final curtain on my dramas. She studied me a long time, dead-pan except for the twinkling eyes. Finally she asked, 'How much?'

A few days later, I gave her an estimate of our monthly income if we liquidated everything. It was a skilful job, taking into account the cost of maintaining a job, the waste of keeping up with the neighbours, the cost of boredom, as well as the more common factors. But that was not what she had asked. So I told her what the dollar value of the whole bundle would be if I committed *hara-kiri* that night.

First she studied the distant wall; then her finger nails. Then she made a long examination of me. Finally, she gave me her choice.

'I can wait. I just can't face breaking in another like you.'

Thus began what was written up in a Sunday magazine as 'The Well Researched Retirement'. After nineteen years and many provings, our pre-plan still works. Anyone can benefit by it. You can start now, if you want to, while you're reading.

Once we were convinced by our dollar figures that we could cut out in three years, we entered limbo. Limbo is an emotional paralysis many undergo on the edge of self-unemployment.

My wife was a Master Librarian. I had access to the company commercial research department. We decided to combine our research experience and develop a system that would fill the awful wait preceding actual retirement.

The pre-plan plan

Step one is making a list of all the things you never want to do again. This is a way of blowing off the frustrations that pile up while you're waiting.

For example:

    never again mow grass
    never again play nursemaid to the neighbour's dogs
    never again drive to the suburban station
    never again see dirty snow in a city.

Whenever you burst out, 'I hope I never again have to ...' you write it down. This becomes your List number 1 **Never-agains**.

It may sound a little childish. It is psychologically sound and not at all childish, as my wife and I found out many times.

Each of you must make this list separately. This is essential! No peeking. No criticising. No 'helping'. It must be absolutely secret, otherwise you ruin all that follows.

After you have built up a dozen or so **Never-agains**, over a couple of weeks, put the list in a drawer to mellow. From time to time you will make additions. You should also make revisions. The list sort of ripens. What happens is you become more objective, taking yourself more seriously. On the other hand, in retrospect, a spate of bad temper may seem not really you, just a tummy ache. The revisions will be the slow realisation of yourself as you move mentally and emotionally toward your hoped-for new life. Gradually your lists will lose their strangeness.

Then is the time to start List number 2.

It is best to begin your lists at the same time, assuming you are a couple retiring together. If you are a single person, you will probably retire with a friend or relative. Treat the other person as a spouse. No sneak previews. No saying, 'Let me share just this one idea with you. It's so silly.'

No!

List number 2 is your **Hope-tos**.

These are more fun than your **Never-agains**. Also more important. Your finished list will reveal what you really want out of life. If you do it right, it can make retirement your most exhilarating years. You face up to what you have been suppressing, postponing, perhaps sacrificing for the sake of someone else. Start with little things.

For example:

walk through low mountains every morning

swim in warm ocean every day

then go back to bed

eat ice cream for breakfast, eggs for dinner.

In time, as you stop being bashful with yourself, your list becomes more serious, such as: get a high school diploma; go back to college; ski six months out of the year, boat the remaining six; take up ballet; have a love affair (come on, be honest with yourself – this is in absolute secrecy).

Keep the list in the drawer, that secret drawer. As the possibility of retirement matures into probability, those **Hope-tos** change from daydreams to the reality of your new future.

Pre-retirement becomes no longer a worrisome wonderment. You have set up a negative and positive approach. A lively current flows through your thoughts.

This is your cue: the time is right for combining your lists. Now you will appreciate the strict secrecy. Exchange your **Never-agains**.

This should be done leisurely when the two of you are not going to be interrupted. Above all, it must be done with mutual respect. We can't give examples to fit everybody, so let's take a few from my list.

My first **Never-again** was: 'I hope I never again attend a cocktail party.'

Her first was: 'I want never again to entertain your clients.'

3

At this point we could have ruined our relationship. Rehashing pent-up annoyances can sabotage retirement plans.

Think what would have happened if she had said, 'Well, if I had known my parties were such a bore all these years, I . . .'

Suppose I had flared up with, 'Why didn't you tell me? I could have taken them to the Club. Didn't mean to . . .'

Now do you see why – no comments!

Combining the private wishes of two people separates the self-absorbed from the mature. Look at the other person's **Never-agains** with compassion; and gratitude. If you never knew she felt that way, realise that your partner buried a feeling, probably out of consideration for you, but, anticipating a new, freer life, does not want to continue hiding it. The **Never-agains** were written under stress. Look for the broad aspect. Find a common denominator with your own.

In fact, my wife and I were saying the same thing from different points of view. We were both tired of phony expense account business parties.

Here are some other **Never-agains**.

Mine was: 'Never again to wear a neck-tie.'

Hers was: 'No more stockings in summer.'

We were both thinking towards casual clothes, an indication of a life style.

Mine: 'Never to say Yes when I feel like saying, You go to hell.'

Hers: 'Never have to pretend to like somebody for purely commercial reasons.'

Soon it became obvious we both wanted a life freed from business hypocrisy. I think we began to admire each other anew – a pleasant beginning for two older folk about to live closer than they had for decades.

Once you have politely perused each other's lists, you should combine them. The resulting document, of what you both want never to do again, can act as a strong guide when you begin looking for your retirement home.

Not all the items on each list will have similar ones to be blended. Nevertheless, be sure to include these unmatched items into the joint list. They are as real to the other person as your peculiarities are real to you.

Now, in your next step, you come right up against the backbone of your tomorrows. Combine your **Hope-tos**.

While you read over the other person's list, remember you are looking at someone's unfulfilled life, a secret trust. Be tactful. Best – just keep quiet.

Suppose a driving executive wants to build sandcastles for six months, don't guffaw at it. He'll get bored in an hour. It only means he feels he has missed his boyhood.

If his sixty-year-old wife admits a yearning to study ballet, don't remind her she's fifty pounds overweight. Ballet may give her the incentive to reduce. And, make note, Mr Executive, over the years you have obviously not been enough incentive.

For instance, here are how our **Hope-tos** did combine.

My first: 'No matter where we go, my wife must be happy.' I was convinced she was less eager to leave our cosy apartment and grand-children than I was. Some sacrifice was involved for my sake.

Her first: 'To become a full-time librarian.' As part of our financial researching, she acquired a brand new Master of Library Science and wanted a nine to five job for the first time in her life.

Our combined first wish was patently: find a library job.

My second was: 'Outdoor swimming all year.'

Her second: 'Live where my husband will be free from arthritic pain.' In those days, I lived under the frequently-heard diagnosis, 'We don't know the cause. We don't know the cure. You'll just have to live with it.'

Our wishes dovetailed from the beginning, after we got the idea of looking for the broad intent. As our number 2 lists fitted together, it became obvious we were both drifting toward the same question: Where?

For those who believe they are already in the best possible place, blessings: heaven is in the heart. You are already in paradise, or, maybe, just dead. For those who decide to move, the 'Where' should be treated with the best of research. It's a quite different kind of job.

Meanwhile, this is a good time for you to start List number 3. Secrecy is over. Share your laughs.

Your third list is: **Jobs-I'm-really-going-to-finish**.

List every horrid little job that has bugged you for the last umpteen years: clean the brass on that antique chest; write out the family tree; paste all the family snapshots into nice albums. That was my wife's. Mine was to put all our records on to cassettes.

Should you expect to finish these tasks? Well, after eighteen years, our photos are still in shoe boxes under the guest bed. The records still take up the whole floor of my wardrobe. Our tasks were not done for the same reason that they were not done in the first place – there was always something more interesting.

However, don't laugh off these endless unfulfilments. They have the value of continuity, when you find the Brave New World of leisure becomes the Frightening New World of disorientation. Incidentally, real estate people advise that the first things to take with you are pictures, bric-à-brac and small rugs. These conserve the emotions of memory better than furniture. People often replace furniture.

Now, if your combined number 1 and 2 lists keep egging you on to get going, your time has come to decide WHERE.

This was where my wife and I fell headlong into our first mistake, probably the most frequent among all retirees. We started to look for a city, with a library and outdoor swimming, but a city where I would never again mow the lawn, where she would not wear stockings, where life was serene. We made no progress.

Then one day, I thought I felt an embryo of common sense. I asked my wife how many dry-cleaning establishments she patronised.

'One. Why?'

'How many drug stores?'

'Two. If I can't get what I want at Miller's, I go – Hey! If you are thinking of opening a shop in your old age, I have one more **Never-again** for *your* list. Me.'

There were 1200 dry cleaners where we lived. And 1400 drug stores. However, the art museum did brag equality with the New York Met.

'How many times in the last ten years have we been to the art museum?' I queried.

She used her fingers but could not stir up more than three.

'Three cocktail parties, because the Curator is a friend of my cousin's aunt.'

So – 1199 dry cleaners and 1398 drug stores were just places in my way as I drove to work. We did not need a city. We needed a library near year-round swimming, in whatever place they both might be.

So here is the rule we had broken: do not look for a place you think you might like. Look for the things to do, which you know you will like.

By the time most people retire, they have been in harness so long – to a job, a contract, to parents, children, a hospital or even an habituated shopping centre, that they can no longer comprehend true freedom. Have you ever seen a draught animal finally released to pasture? It may stand for hours not knowing where to go.

Well, here's a little trick to get you out of the pasture. It worked well for us. It has worked for others over the years. Go together to a quiet place away from people. Imagine yourself out in space. Look back at the world. Look back at life on earth, all of it, everywhere, in winter slush and summer sweat. Now think what you hope to find – out there. That's what you hope for, isn't it – a new life out of this world!

Now believe this: you can live anywhere you can afford if it suits you. For a while this may make you want to hide under the bed. Eventually, the out-of-this-world freedom will help you skip over the tedious gabble about one likes mountains but the other prefers the seashore.

Remind yourself of what your combined List number 2 said you both wanted. Stay with that idea.

We came up with Florida, the Mediterranean, Northern Mexico, the Bahamas, Bermuda (at that time we were not sure whether the Bahamas were in Bermuda or vice versa), the Caribbean, Arizona, Lower California, San Diego, Ceylon. Our list would take a lifetime to explore.

Then we checked ourselves against our list. Here, my wife developed a late-born **Never-again**. She didn't want to die trying to whisper through her oxygen tent in a foreign language. On the other hand, I had noted that I enjoy burbling around in a few words of this and that.

Incidentally, this tiny **Hope-to** of mine about languages, not matched by a similar **Hope-to** from my wife, fourteen years later proved to be the key to a whole new life. It got me out of the slough of widowerhood. Don't sell your little 'sillies' short.

After we struck off the foreign language places, out went the Mediterranean, the Canaries, Mexico, Ceylon. Of course, the cold water entrants went too – Canada, San Francisco and virtually all of North America.

Finally, for us, the wheel stopped at the Caribbean, but the big question was unanswered: do people under palm trees carry library cards? Looking back now, it was an utterly stupid question, but neither of us had been to the Caribbean. Of course, my wife did some preliminaries on libraries, which only wetted the bookworm in her.

Our heretofore perfunctory holidays took on the urgency of adventure. Far from having pre-retirement slumps and qualms, our researched pre-planning took on the aspect of an exciting race. Find the library before my company handed me that scuba diving watch I knew they were keeping for the farewell party.

In two trips, we picked an island. In the joyous flurry, we made our second, and worst, mistake. We contracted palm tree fever. We revelled in glorious, romantic, idyllic vacations. Our paradise had nothing to do with libraries, with retirement costs or with our well researched pre-plan.

When we finally woke up after a near-miss at buying land, we learned that my American wife could not get a work permit on this Dutch island.

So, here's another rule for you: do not mix vacationing with looking for a home site.

Be sure you learn the worst when you are seeking a location. Question, interview, probe – investigate the bad. Then all surprises will be good. A real estate salesperson once told me to see a house in the midst of the worst storm in years. She said if I liked it then, I'd love it ever after. I went. I did. She was right.

It's common sense. Don't concentrate on a good time at a resort when you are looking for a home. Look for the worst. You are not going to be on vacation for the rest of your life. You are going to be on Social Security. Maybe penicillin.

There are bushels of cases who retired with palm tree fever, or golf course fever, or ski chalet fever and after a few years divorced, crumpled and went back.

In the first year when we were settled in our new home, two typical examples of retirement-collapse occurred.

The mayor of a small US town continued his construction business on the island. He was well-adjusted, doing his own thing but in a better climate. He built a beautiful home. In a short time, his wife cracked up and went back. Ostensibly, the reason was she could not get the morning paper delivered in time for her coffee, as she had for decades. Those who knew her well said it was because she was no longer 'Madam Mayoress'. In fact, she had become a mere immigrant. The semi-happy ending is that he returned with her.

Another wife was sewing a blue dress. She ran out of thread and on the whole island could not get a matching spool. She left. But her husband had never been so in love as he was with his new boat. He stayed. They divorced.

Hold on to your combined lists. They can guide you through rapidly changing conditions. The **Never-agains** are a scale against which to test your environment. The **Hope-tos** are your true values undistorted by the limitations of a life-style you wanted to leave; undistorted also by the fleeting social conditions you experience while making new 'friends', many of whom you may never see again.

Even years later, whether you moved or not, your lists may prove to be your best confidants. Time can come even in retirement when you need a reminder of what kind of person you really want to be.

A daughter may present you with an unexpected grandchild. A son may telephone from a police station – he's so sorry. The inescapable will certainly hit you: your partner dies. These traumas can derail you. Eventually, those few sentences of clear thinking written in the buoyancy of optimistic pre-planning pulled me back on track.

After Fran's death, I had no course, no purpose. Five years slumped by in apathy before I came across our combined **Hope-tos**. Recall, we recommended that you put in your peculiarities, even if your partner's did not match.

There was the reminder of my old loves of languages and horses.

I decided to go to Mexico, one of the places that got scratched by Frances' last minute **Never-again**. In Mexico, I learned to enjoy some activities I earlier swore I'd never do. I found new friends as well. I was launched into a whole new life because of that little nudge from a long ago **Hope-to**. It hasn't been a bad life, either.

My one example serves to confirm the need for your secrecy. Friends and family not retiring with you will introduce their own input which may drag your whole effort off target. Consider what happened when I confided to my best friend (yes, all the mistakes have been tested– I made them) that I was thinking of the Caribbean. He screamed, 'Sharks!' We were lunching in the Cleveland Athletic Club dining room. Half the men jumped out of their chairs. I just about fell through mine. I checked out sharks. They swim up one side of the Atlantic and down the other. Off New Jersey they pup. So much for sharks in the Caribbean.

The next time I mentioned the Caribbean (I'm a slow learner), he howled 'Hurricanes!' So we ran hurricanes through the Research Department. Hurricanes do originate in the Caribbean, often too far west to affect any islands. They hit the coast of Connecticut twice as often as any Caribbean country, and hit Florida and Texas five times as often.

Why my friend's hysteria? He was technically blind; no beautiful underwater sights for him. Also, his wife was immobile.

When I telephoned my most protective relative to tell her that we were moving to the West Indies, she shouted, 'You can't!' I asked whether she knew where the West Indies were. She didn't. Incidentally, we saw our relatives more often when they were 1200 air miles away than when they were 500 traffic miles.

If you decide to use this pre-plan, keep it secret.

And remember, always research the worst; don't mix a vacation with looking for real estate. The good will present itself. Do not look for a place, rather look for what you want to do. Then don't move until you can't resist going. Never run away from a place. Always run to it.

If your mind is running towards the Caribbean, the rest of this book will guide you into the seas and shores that are burgeoning as a coveted living area. By the nature of the Caribbean, it should always be blessed with the sweetest air, washed by four thousand miles of Atlantic. Its small islands without mineral resources are not suited to industry. They are just about ideal for tourism or for year-round, dream-come-true living. Beauty is everywhere. Population densities are low. The peoples are pleasant, for generations free with living easy in what probably is the most benign climate in the world, yet with all modern amenities, even to telephones that don't work. Their heritage has given them a sense of hospitality toward newcomers.

Keep in mind that an increase is projected for world population — two billion more in the next twenty years. Where are the great unoccupied areas to receive this additional one third? Siberia; Western China; Northern Canada; the Brazilian jungles; various deserts; or the Caribbean? Resale is little problem, whether condo or private house.

Of all these beckoning areas, the Caribbean has the most direct transportation from Britain, Canada, Europe and the US.

The mere demand for land in the next twenty years suggests the Caribbean as a good investment. Furthermore, ever since OPEC kicked up their heels and prices, the cost of living in the sunny, sandy, surfy Caribbean has been going down, relative to the continents. The whole Caribbean, once considered expensive for average retirees, has become comparatively cheaper. In Chapter Ten we give specific figures. They necessarily require personal adjustments, which is why they have been located after you know a little more about the region. If you want to start roughing out probable costs, don't forget to include these items.

Parts of your post-retirement budget

1 Cost of holding a job
2 Cost of keeping up appearances
3 Cost of fighting climate
4 Cost of
   a) food – cold weather menu
   b) transport – long distances
   c) clothes – cold weather type, fashion pressure
5 Cost of boredom
6 Cost of reduced health
7 Compound interest reinvested versus part-time earnings from rentals or condo commitment

When these items are viewed dispassionately in all their ramifications, the total can be surprising.

In Chapter Ten, *Cost of Living*, all these categories are examined in detail. There are also recent figures on the usual categories people always ask about, as well as an overall method for guesstimating.

There is one more factor in the future growth of the Caribbean. It will never get over being called 'an influential, political and financial Basin'. That to a geographic region is like calling a middle-aged woman 'a Dish'.

A long and happy retirement to you both. Now turn the page and be zoomed out of this world!

TWO
Off the earth again

We will not go so far this time. Just far enough to see how huge the Caribbean is – about half the size of the whole United States.

From Mexico's Yucatan down through Central America, it stretches the entire coast of South America – Panama, Columbia, Venezuela. These nations are all well integrated, conscious of their cultural identities. This west/south Caribbean is not what we will look at for your current investment or eventual retirement.

At the northeast tip of Venezuela is Trinidad, the southern-most island of a chain which curves north about midway in the Atlantic between Mexico and Africa. The chain veers abruptly westwards to Cuba, almost back to Yucatan. These little islands enclose the northeast Caribbean. They are already bustling with retirees and condoers.

Most come from Britain, Canada and the US, but also from Holland, France, Germany, Scandinavia and a few from all over. Some investment money comes even from Taiwan and a large oil tank farm from Arabia. It was bruited not long ago that some strange bedfellows from Algeria, Libya, Syria, Iraq *et al.* had a yen for an airport. All the world endorses our choice of the exciting, provocative, important Caribbean Basin.

The west/south nations are crystallized in their ways, their morals, their sense of rightness. They are Spanish proud. It is possible for you to retire there – as an immigrant. No matter how you tried to identify with the customs, you would always carry the stigma of polite rejection as an '*imigrante*'. Immigrant blemish is the same the world over – except in the east/north Caribbean islands.

This probably is the most distinctive phenomenon of the region.

The crux is that the limits of a continental country are connected by land. Islands are connected by water. Land people think water separates islands. Between islands, water is the superhighway. Kings were able to close harbours and destroy forts – but never to imprison the sea. For hundreds of years the kings of Europe paid war debts with islands. Innocent little Tobago changed kings thirty-one times because it had the misfortune of being strategic. St Lucia in the seventeen hundreds went between England and France like a ping-pong ball. Sometimes the switch meant little more than changing the flag and the garrison at the fort for a few months. However the French king did pull a fast one over the English which has lasted until today. He got back Martinique in exchange for 'a vast expanse of worthless ice called Canada'.

Beneath this crust of European quarrelling, a growing population of native islanders evolved their own firm character. If a change of kingship resulted in no supplies from the new, or the old, mother country for months, the islanders went off at night via their sea highways to exchange goods with relatives on nearby islands. Life went on as usual. Officially such actions were called smuggling. Islanders considered it simple survival. The attitude of letting outsiders have their foibles gradually became a regional characteristic. Today it is advocated as a psychiatrically sound mood – acceptance.

The simple pragmatism of Caribbean smuggling was taught me when I had been in the islands less than a year. It was ebony dark when the *Maverick* lay at anchor in a cove on St Lucia. Trucks without lights suddenly rumbled down a dirt road to the beach. Small boats, with outboards muffled, came from the sea. Feet scuffled on the beach. The boats retreated. The trucks gunned into high and fled.

Captain Jack Carstarphen explained without interest, 'Probably provisioning a big hotel. Tax-free liquor from St Barts. Or they bought from Barbados with the fifty-cent dollar.'

Jack had cruised the islands for many years.

Curiosity kept me quizzing our first mate. He was from St Vincent. After several days he seemed to think me safe for a proposal.

Anguilla, he said, built the best native sloops. His cousins would build me one for $36 000 EC, $18 000 US. We would make two runs with rum, clearing visibly at customs on St Thomas. Then a night run to the north coast with cargo costing $20 000 US, sell it for $40 000 US, tax free.

The skipper, crew and I would split the liquor profit three ways. Profit from the sale of the boat would be mine, less 10% to the skipper for expediting the arrangement.

When I declined the offer, nothing I could say was understandable to the Vincentian. His was a simple deal, performed many times, standard procedure. Everybody knew certain dealers on St Thomas made night buys. Besides, it was a good thing to do. For the crew it was their once-in-a-lifetime chance to get into business and off the deck. He could see only one reason why I refused: I did not trust him personally. We were never friends afterwards.

You would expect insularity, yet Caribbean islands know a cosmopolitan undercurrent. Each is in sight of several others. A West Indian is aware that on one his people are thinking in English, on another in Dutch, on a third in Spanish or perhaps in English and French interchangeably. Meanwhile his own lingua franca, West Indian Creole, is basic on all. That makes for tolerance.

This is the atmosphere for Caribbean living. Not *imigrantes* but rather immediate membership in a deeply blended society which takes for granted and appreciates variations among newcomers. You will be judged as a person: a polite person or a not polite person; not as a yank or a limey or whatever your foreignness.

Although the Caribbean will always be a water world, this book will not go into boating. So many books have already detailed the coasts and marinas; here, there is neither space nor need to repeat.

Nor shall the book cover the vagaries of getting a job. This is about investment, although some retirees do find work. That, too, needs a separate volume. We will see the Caribbean through the eyes of a runaway to new life. Tourists may protest at each page, 'It isn't that way at all! I never saw it so.' Quite!

Developers, exploiters and opportunists will see it differently, too. Some with no hesitation will 'improve' to their own tastes. Some will milk it as absentee landlords. Others gather booty and leave behind wreckage. They are the modern-day pirates; they are not retirees.

Framed on the wall of a delightful inn call *Posada de Aldea*, at San Miguel de Allende, Guanajuato, Mexico, is a credo for good travellers. It is here adapted for good retirees, about to start island hopping.

Ten commandments for new-comers

1 Thou shalt not expect to find things as thou hast them at home, for thou hast left thy home to find things different.
2 Thou shalt not take anything too seriously for a carefree mind is the beginning of a fine retirement.
3 Thou shalt not let other people get on thy nerves, for thou art paying good money for a good time.
4 Remember thy visa so that thou knowest where it is at all times.
5 Remember to take only half the clothes you think you need and twice the amount of money.
6 Remember, if we were expected to stay in one place we would have been created with roots.
7 Thou shalt not worry. He that worrieth hath no pleasure. Few things are ever fatal.
8 Thou shalt not judge the people of a country by the person with whom thou hast had trouble.
9 Thou shalt not make thyself too obviously American, British or Canadian. 'When in Rome do somewhat as the Romans do.'
10 Remember thou art a guest in every land and that he that treateth his host with respect shall in turn be treated as an honoured guest.

This island-hopping chapter can be but a nibble: and so, with a wistful nod at beautiful but lost Cuba, let us start with Hispaniola.

HAITI shares the magnificent green mountains flowing right out to the white beaches of Hispaniola with the Dominican Republic. Something of Graham Greene's Tonton Macoutes lingered in my memory as I entered Port au Prince airport. The usual amorphous mass of passengers swarmed toward a row of card tables where men sat examining passports. Shabby makeshift, I thought. Sixteen young men and women tall and slender suddenly materialised. Their egg yellow shirts and black pants enhanced their ebony complexions – certainly they must have been chosen for beauty and grace. Like dancers they gestured the passengers into lines at each table. If one line grew to more than five, the extras were drawn smoothly to another. The performance was a ballet of efficiency. Bebe Doc was not using Papa's shoes.

By the time I reached the street I was smitten with Haiti's blend of Afro-Gallic insouciance. Even a beggar approached as though bearing an invitation to a soirée. Nor did this pleasant manner fade when I declined.

Despite their poverty Haitians glow with pride. They alone beat Napoleon without help. They founded the second republic of the New World without help. They have a saying, 'No Haitian has a small penis. Just that some have trousers too tight.'

Entranced with Port au Prince I became lost, with the problem that my French is *sehr schlect* as well as *muy poco*. Puckering for my best effort at Gallic accent, I asked a policeman, 'Good morning, Sir. Please, where is the Tourist Bureau?'

The gendarme stared ahead. I got the side of the face for as long as I could take it. That was all I got. I philosophised: there are xenophobic jackasses everywhere. Even the idolised Greeks must have had a few or we would not know how to say *xenophobia*. Assuaged with this trifle of élitism, I hurried to the next policeman.

'*Bonjour, Monsieur. S'il vous plaît, où est le Bureau du Tourism?*'

This cop stared straight ahead. Side of the face! Then I noticed the lips working as only a Frenchman can masticate speech before ejecting it. Slowly he regurgitated my question. '*Où est le Bureau du Tourism?*'

I waited for him to cud his answer. He repeated the question, elaborating. I thought he even mimicked my intonation.

That popped me. I'm dedicated to keeping the Caribbean wholesome. On wings of rage, I located the Bureau du Tourism and its startled clerk. He heard to the last rasp my monologue on xenophobia, skin colour obsession and general Gallic snottiness.

'Oh, Monsieur! We do not ask information from our gendarmes. They do not speak French – hardly any of them. They are not educated. Just village talk. That one was repeating what you said to let you know he understood your question but he could not explain to you. He gave you the best he knows.'

Crawling back under a rock, I said that hereafter I would ask my questions in a shop.

'Oh, do not do that! Not in a shop! They will charge you for the information. Look carefully at the men on the street. Select a well dressed man, you know, educated with a good job. He will not, you know ... Ask a man like that.'

Haiti needs more time. She deserves visitors who know Haiti better than Haiti knows herself. With harshness she could be hurt.

Besides, you would need strong personal reasons to retire there.

Let's cross the border into Dominican Republic, no more like Haiti than a springbok is like a panda. Cross carefully, the Dominican Republic is not welcoming to Haitian refugees.

The DOMINICAN REPUBLIC is blessed with the highest mountains in this part of the Caribbean, a wealth of natural resources, rain, fertility – magnificence. Currently it is making an admirable attempt to accommodate tourism. In 1971 the government enacted a programme of laws to favour tourists which also covers retirees: incentives; protection for foreign capital and investments; control against speculation. All the island governments seem to awaken first to tourism because the results of their efforts are clearly visible and tourism brings quick money, albeit much flows out again skimmed to outside investors. This is not the result with retiree expenditure. Retirees stay on the island.

Today there is already a 'part-time' population in the Dominican Republic, mostly Anglos who own homes and spend the winter there. Some European or Asian expatriates have formed colonies. A small group of South Americans are attracted by the charm, the stability and low costs. (See Chapter Ten, *Cost of Living*.)

Now for the ambience for settling. You know how heritage subtly influences a whole class of people, generation to generation — the Mayflower syndrome. The Dominican Republic was settled by Columbus; in person. Then by his son; in person. From here sailed Cortes, Balboa, Pizarro, Bartolmé, Velasquez to conquer over half the New World, before Hudson went to find his river.

Nevertheless, if you like grandeur at a bargain price and can garble a smattering of *espanol*, the anticipated boom in the Caribbean points to Dominican Republic as a gracious host and a good bet at least for a long visit.

PUERTO RICO is another intensively Spanish country but no longer monolithic. It is on the multilingual edge where the Caribbean starts to dilute deep rooted Spanish culture. Puerto Rico has a dual character. Thousands of visitors passing through San Juan airport get no true impression of the whole island. Imagine drawing a conclusion about the whole state of New York from an airport in NY City. The first thing you would pack would be a gas mask.

Puerto Rico employs many statesiders, nevertheless it is nearly virgin territory for true retirees; ideal for transition from urban sprawl to subtropic spaciousness. Someone who is not sure he can survive the decompression would find interior Puerto Rico restful yet exciting. Tourists do not meet Puerto Ricans of their own economic and educational level. The stereotype of Puerto Rico comes from the landless, jobless emigrants. As one well schooled Puerto Rican exclaimed, 'All they ever talk with are taxi drivers and airport personnel!'

A mere thirty miles east from San Juan airport is Fajardo. This is a twin personality village. Imagine Miami Beach plunked down on the coast of Nova Scotia. Fajardo is the gateway between sophisticated northern Puerto Rico and an exactly opposite world of central and southern Puerto Rico.

The old village of Fajardo wears its heart on its beach, a row of fishing boats drawn up waiting for dawn. On the heights above, you can tell the one-room, open front grocery shops from the open front bars by the radios blasting. On the rim of this rural setting, thirty-floor towers of nth degree luxury sprout skyward with startling incongruity. Soaring condos are footed not on underground garages but in private marinas with the tenants' umpteen thousand dollar sports craft parked freeboard to freeboard. One cluster of towers sits on a miniscule island of its own in the harbour. Tenants commute to the mainland on their own ferry, a sort of Thoreau in white tie and tails.

The road from Fajardo squirms up to the cordillera, 100 miles of magnificent 5000 foot mountains. Small inns, an easy day's drive apart, punctuate the Scenic Route which runs the length of the island. Many reclaim distinctive quarters – an old coffee plantation or converted mansions – inexpensive, supervised by the government, patronised by local people of the calibre retirees would be glad to meet. Such mountains are not suspected at the airport: there are primordial ferns as tall as cocopalms, gigantic bamboos lacing branches into lofty Gothic arches above the highway. The south coast parallels the cordillera only thirty miles away. Between mountains and coast lie rolling hills then flat sugar-cane expanses dropping off to ranchlike fields where Puerto Rican cowboys herd cattle. This mini-world where it is as if the foothills of the Rockies were minutes from the ranch lands of Colorado, the cane-fields of Louisiana all edged by a shoreline of fishing villages and lobster eating spots like Maine, is only three hours from the Washington/Boston megalopolis.

Island ambience

Definitely Caribbean yet not West Indies. You never leave the US flag, money, prices, standards. Minimum risk, wonderfully healthy environment, unexcelled for variety in only 35 by 100 miles. It couldn't be easier to go back. If nothing pleases you on this versatile, exotic land, perhaps you had better play Kansas City or Manchester for openers.

THE US VIRGINS, twenty minutes flight east, have had so much written about them that only a retiree's point of view is left to explore. The USVI offer the famed climate with minimum change of American social climate: same language (even with recent Spanish incursion), money, banks, social security, medicare. Only Federal income tax: no state, county, municipal, sales, school or sewer taxes. Real estate tax is lower. Land is available on all three islands, on St Thomas sometimes at bargain rates — $8000 to $9000 a $\frac{1}{4}$ acre but without a view and probably in a valley with little breeze. Land sales currently are brisk, but not house sales. People are tending to trade up to more expensive properties after they learn island values.

Population density on ST THOMAS is about 50 000 on 39 useable square miles: lower on St Croix with about three times as much land. Population statistics need to be viewed as evanescent. The number of illegal aliens varies but, except during depressed years, it is high. Ex-Governor Evans addressing a public relations group a decade ago, said the number sometimes reached ten thousand.

The flood of humanity from cruise ships often equals the resident population of Charlotte Amalie, St Thomas' one town. The south coast is congested. The north is graced with impressive homes and estates and a theatrically superb view all the way to the end of the British Virgins. Daily radio welcomes to cruise ships warn residents how big a crowd will glut Main Street. Residents learn to go down-town when ships are fewest.

ST CROIX has a much lower population density, fewer cruise ships, overall less congestion. It has two small cities. Christiansted is usually considered one of the two most beautiful cities in the

Caribbean, with St Georges, Grenada. Housing costs about 5% less than St Thomas, but crime may be a little higher. Two large industries affect the temper of the island, one by employing workers from the oil industry who do not always harmonise with Caribbean characteristics.

The tempo of St Croix is a little easier, more suburban. St Thomas always has been a commercial island, with many plantation owners maintaining town houses. Both islands are rich in cultural affairs compared with the 'downislands' farther east. St Croix is less 'West-Indiany'. On St Croix the ballet, theatre and literary groups feel more like art for art's sake: St Thomas — art for native expression. St Croix is a paragon of investment diversity, especially Carambola.

Retirees on ST JOHN are not so subjected to obsession with tourist dollars. Demand for land is up even though the National Park has first rights to buy any becoming available within the assigned park limits. The life for residents is one of elegant quietude set by the high standards of National Park and of Caneel Bay, a typical superior Rockresort spread. Unless you own your own boat, your route to St Thomas' shopping will be through Cruz Bay, which is a village growing without quality control. Nevertheless St Johnians act like any suburban people: glad to get home and kick off their shoes.

Island ambience

The US Virgins offer investment in three descending tempos, St Thomas, St Croix, St John; a transplanted mainland life in an exciting water world for the slight deterrent of higher food prices. You can feel the constant effort of some of the transplantees to counteract the unconscious – and often conscious – effort of others to divide the population into blacks and whites, We and Them. If you are comfortable with attitudes and social stress on the continent, you can be more than comfortable in the US Virgins.

TORTOLA is the British Virgin nearest St John, about eight miles, give or take a few tugs on the oars. Enterprising BV Islanders have rowed to the US at night on diverse West Indian-type missions. The two countries are the same geographic archipelago. Although a sincere friendship exists, they are different from each other in just about the same way that Britain differs from the US. British Virgins are smaller, drier, quieter and, until the late 1960s, 'undiscovered' because tourists were few. They use US money, and have US currency on their stamps with the Queen's profile. The Queen's photo is in post office and clinic. The British get dressed (meaning long sleeves and shoes) and have a jolly band show on June 16th, the official birthday of the sovereign. Americans are invited. Americans stay up late and make a lot of noise on July 4th. The British smile and look away. Everybody flies the Union Jack.

I once asked a shopkeeper, whose mien and moustache bespoke Fleet Street, whether the increasing flow of visitors from the USVI tempted him to replace the Union Jack with Old Glory.

'Nevah! When visitors step off the boat they see here a small St Thomas of twenty years ago. That's nostalgia. Then they see the Union Jack. They feel they have travelled. We will always be British!'

The gentleman failed to note that Mamma Britain makes handsome grants in aid annually to her territory for such capital improvements as roads and schools.

Tortola has all the government and commerce of this mini-country, and Road Town, the only approximation of a village with about 6000 steadies plus part-timers in comfortable, non-ostentatious homes on the steep hillsides.

No. 2 island is VIRGIN GORDA, half an hour by boat, about four minutes by plane. Virgin Gorda is to Tortola an exclusive, expensive suburb, *sans* industry, *sans* rush, *sans* grubbiness. Virgin Gorda is 8.3 square miles of tourism and retireeism, top quality in its hotel, inns and yachting. Wherever you are is close to a beach. The island is enjoying a boom; but housing gets more expensive all the time. (See Chapter Ten for costs.)

ANEGADA is fifteen miles north, flat, sandy, with colossal beaches but nothing else. About two decades ago, Anegada was the target of massive exploitation. The natives with eloquent simplicity and typical common sense, appealed to the Crown and got it squelched. It is on the verge of being opened for outsiders but land is not yet (1989) available in quantity.

Tiny JOST VAN DYKE is doing some wishful thinking that will make it a grade A settlement spot once it acquires services. So far there are no part-timers or retirees but there is some attractive hillside land. It is a few minutes' boat ride to Tortola for all supplies and travel.

Island ambience

The 1980 census was 11 152 locals, plus, from the US and its territories, 528; from UK, 310; others (Canadians, Scandinavians mostly), 363. This does not include aliens from Commonwealth Caribbean islands. The total population in 1983 pushed 13 000. The government shows no favouritism among continental expatriates.

The serene life becomes disturbed by the need to shop on St Thomas or Puerto Rico. Actually Tortola has more than retirees expect but the little shops look like World War I general stores and are not fully explored by retirees. Newcomers return from hub island shopping with the oath. 'I'll never leave here again!' Old-timers (five years or more) are complaining, 'This place is spoiled. Too many people!'

Over 300 Am-Brit-Cans have work permits. Over 100 more are self-employed. Government slows construction by making work permits for down-island aliens hard to get. Over-employment is a policy to keep the country from unemployment. It is difficult to get help but so soothing to live among natives who feel secure. There is hardly any thieving.

Before we jump the 110 miles of Anegada Passage to the true West Indies, there are two disparate, distinguished countries in this north-central region: The Caymans and Jamaica.

The three petite CAYMANS, 480 miles south of Miami, have been a British Crown Colony since they separated from Jamaica in 1959. No other Caribbean islands are remotely like them, from what man has done. We are offering here only an introduction. If you like the handshake, write to the Chamber of Commerce, Box 1000, Grand Cayman, Cayman Islands. Ask for the *Real Estate Review* and *Fact Sheet No. One*. Their promotion literature is expert.

The 1979 census put the total population at 16 677. Expatriates numbered 3203; the proportions: UK 20.71%, US 17.6%, Canadians 1.9%. Others amounted to 59.8% of whom 39.8% were Jamaicans. These figures do not include foreigners who have acquired Cayman status. The Cayman presentation of itself is refreshingly grown-up: 'Over expansion has created an inflated work force. Housing is short. Rents high.'

However, the islands do have impressive condominiums exquisitely architected.

The Caymans are being developed with the most erudite financial acumen. They are a corporate executive's daydream of where to retire without loss of identity.

Beach land values increased per foot of frontage from $50 US in 1959 to $10 000 in 1980.

Most islands are still trying to get roads paved and telephones that operate. Grand Cayman has installed a Public Paging System. An operator can pass a message to anyone anywhere on the island who has a pager: direct dialling to Canada and the US is immediately available.

Quoting further from the government's self-definition: 'There is not and never has been a casino-type economy.' Strict licensing laws control the sale of liquor. There is no direct taxation, except 'a small poll tax'. If you do not know what a poll tax is for, ask an American from below the Mason and Dixon line.

If you have qualms about the security of your retirement funds, you can put your sock to rest in the Caymans. Their cheques will get you anywhere. You may find peace of mind from a financial contact on a Cayman while you take with you only what you need for your grass hut and bare feet elsewhere.

JAMAICA, only 178 miles south by southeast from Grand Cayman, has for centuries been the mirror of stately England in the Caribbean. In fact, the upper crust has been analysed, and accused, as identifying with all things English to such an extent that the less affluent felt (and until very recently – feel) like Jamaicans without a Jamaica. The clash created a schism wherein the seeds of socialism were sowed, sorrowfully. Jamaica, now the prodigal son, has returned to free enterprise with a programme for rejuvenation that is a model for the world.

For example, you would expect a programme aimed at fighting crime to concentrate on the police. Jamaica's does to the extent that the police are to be rendered immune to political control. But note these revisions related to crime extirpation: creating two Youth Development Centres in each parish for training and guidance of the erstwhile neglected rural youngsters; less obsessive concentration favouring the tourist areas; a programme for upgrading over 200 rural towns by improving schools, health centres, community centres, fire and police services, as well as roads, water and electricity supplies. Crime is already decreasing; unemployment, however, is high. People still lock cars and houses against petty theft.

The total complex of programmes for the regeneration of Jamaica's physical, commercial and social existence shows a depth of psychological insight into modern therapy usually left by governments to philanthropy groups.

Too big a gap between the indigenous haves and have-nots caused the breakdown. Now the cause is admitted and attacked.

The government statement is that retirees are welcomed by Jamaica today. The impression you get from booklets, *Investing in Jamaica, Moving to Jamaica* and *Starting and Operating a Business in Jamaica* is that you can depend on their word. Write to the Chamber of Commerce, Kingston.

One hundred and ten miles from the British Virgins is Anguilla.

ANGUILLA, one of the few non-volcanic islands, is only 213 feet above sea level at its highest point. It provides no theatre, no commendable nightlife, no casino. Guide books have difficulty finding something to offer. But Anguilla has beaches — man, oh man, does it have beaches! And new resorts! But the greatest attraction for those who want to live there are people you love. In 1967, Anguilla seceded from St Kitts-Nevis after years of gentle discontent. There was talk about St Kitts invading. St Kitts didn't have anything to invade with. The Anguilla police got tired of waiting and stopped watching.

At this time an American dug up a small cannon on his beach. He mounted it facing the sea, jokingly 'to repel invaders'. St Kitts whipped up a fine account of guns on Anguilla which grew into American gangsters taking over the island.

Fifteen Anguillans appointed themselves a peace-keeping committee. By contribution they raised $10 000 to finance a government. News of the American gangsters brought a drop of British paratroopers. It was summer. The ladies, who gathered to see who was dropping in, felt sorry for 'those poor boys so hot in their silly woollen clothes'. They made pitchers of lemonade for the young men.

The soldiers did all sorts of nice things like making a road, improving the harbour and building a recreation centre for everybody. They fell in love with the Anguillan people. Everybody does. On St Thomas we knew a builder who would hire only Anguillans because they were 'more intelligent, more reliable, more cooperative and worked harder'.

This anecdote typifies life on Anguilla.

Anguilla is not for many people, thank God, because there is not much of it, only 36 square miles. You have to be self-sufficient emotionally. You need to value quiet as one values music; to reach out to beauty as one reaches for food; to want to see earth and sky and sea in their entireties. You need to be nice to others, never mind that people haven't much money. It's enough to bring back Sigmund Romberg.

Island ambience

About 55 Americans, 32 British and 3 Canadians own houses on Anguilla. (Remember, there are others who do not own their houses.) Land is available from individuals, not from the government. Beach hotels; not condos. *Cost of Living* is detailed in Chapter Ten.

Outsiders are building at the rate of ten houses a year. A few have generators but the island makes its own electricity. There are telephones. Rentals are available. Given a chance to vote for independence, Anguilla remained a Crown Colony. For real estate information write to Mr Douglas Stott, PO Box 2, The Valley. For other information write to CL Petty, Permanent Minister's Office, The Valley, Anguilla, WI.

Necessities you can buy on Anguilla. For luxuries you have to go to Sint Maarten, twelve miles by plane or boat daily. Actually it is less trouble, backache or pocketbook ache than by train or bus from many a suburb into the city centre. Sint Maarten is a genuine freeport.

In the islands south of Anguilla you see the Caribbean pattern repeated again and again: different nationalities adjacent but commingling easily in their daily routines. A perfect example for the rest of the squabbling world.

SINT MAARTEN shares the island of St Martin with the French St Martin (pronounced San Mahtan). The Dutch side, the smaller though more developed, was picture postcard Dutch tropical with tiny houses swathed in gingerbread fretwork. Philipsburg was and is one of the few booming towns that retained its beach for the length of the town. This is a dominant feature in Caribbean 'progress'. Those towns which pave their main waterfront beach into a broad highway belting out the sea immediately lose much of their romantic flavour. When Sint Maarten lurched into massive tourist-casino development in the late 1960s, Philipsburg retained much of its pre-boom charm.

All the Dutch islands are genuine freeports with no customs houses. This tends to create an environment of 'smart money'. Sint Maarten is heavy with condominiums, congealed along the southeast shore. Where permanent resident expatriates have settled they predominantly gather in enclaves. Sint Maarten in its casino, resort, and resident developments maintains as uniformly high level of living standard as any in the Caribbean, yet, surprisingly, still with a lingering trace of small West Indian island personality, due as much as anything to the Dutch protection of the beaches.

On a small island heavy in condominiums, casinos and the transient population of resort hotels, the aspect of Euro-North Americans is more dominant than the presence of expatriate homeowners. Also the impact is strong of non-West Indians who have lived on the island so long that they are 'permanent residents' rather than expatriates. All the Dutch side of St Martin emanates a cosmopolitan international aura. The Big Spenders fly into St Maarten for the casino life. Mostly they stay in the all-services hotels, use the swimming pools and are flown out, hardly touched by the loveliness of the island. Still, where a large amount of an island's income is derived from gambling and tourism, the outlook of the government, and of the community services, is affected. Islands that are tip-top tourist spots do not necessarily provide what retirees need. How many times a year will you buy a freeport watch?

Because of the duty-free shopping and low price produce from Holland, the cost of rapid expansion is somewhat offset. For any who want to continue in the fast lane but with sailboats on the highway: Sint Maarten.

Saba and St Eustatius – Statia to her friends – are two mountain tops within St Maarten's orb. Both these islets are in effect exclusively residential suburbs for Sint Maarten, ideal if you want the idyllic.

Think of the three as about thirty miles apart, visible just on the horizon with daily commuter service by plane or boat. Expatriates choosing Saba or Statia would want simplicity, health, tranquillity. Weekly shopping on Sint Marten would be either a bloody bore or a little giddy with an afternoon cocktail on the terrace of Seaview overlooking Philipsburg Bay while waiting for the return boat.

SABA is five square miles of mountain top, falling precipitously down to not one beach. Its three villages of Dutch gingerbread toy houses are Dutch clean and West Indian friendly. The people are honest, industrious, courteous, appreciative of nature and highly individualistic. Every morning women holystone their front steps and sweep the street. I once watched the jail being torn down because it had not been used and they wanted something more useful.

Island ambience

Typical of the social life is that in 1970, the Year of the Woman, Saba sent two representatives to a Convention on Curaçao on the subject of Women. This was the first time that a woman had left Saba for any purpose other than to shop or visit relatives. The returned delegates fed the women's organisation such ideas that new laws were passed, completely with the male cooperation, which stated a woman who has money of her own no longer needs her husband's approval to buy an appliance larger than a toaster. Also, a husband, drunk or sober, could no longer sell his wife's possessions without her permission. Either you love Saba on sight or sit on the airstrip waiting for the return plane.

Among Saba's thousand residents, twenty Americans own houses. About half live there all year round. As on all the islands, some expatriates own a car. About $65 000 will put you in residence. See *Cost of Living* in Chapter Ten.

ST EUSTATIUS, a little south from Saba, seven and a half square miles, is two mountain cones with a valley between and one town. The island lacks spectacular forest, rocks or water. It is mainly fields, the slopes of an old volcano and a town that is still much as it was at the time of the American Revolution. Yet Statia -- the land, the town, the coast, the people -- is peculiarly awake. This is particularly odd considering that the whole place was assumed dead for a couple of centuries. It suffered from its own history. It was allegedly, though incorrectly, totally destroyed and never rebuilt. In 1969 the St Maarten Tourist Bureau advised me not to go there because 'there is nothing there'. Such advice has always triggered me to an immediate visit.

With an underwater camera I found the remains of the huge break-water that made Statia the 'Golden Rock' of the Dutch Caribbean empire. Some of the houses from the seventeen hundreds were not only just as they had been, they were inhabited as they had been. The walls and garden spaces of public buildings were exciting. Along the beach stood the remains of the great warehouses where the Dutch stashed war materials captured from the English to smuggle to the rebellious colonies.

Island ambience

Homesites had stood utterly dormant for twelve years when the articles in northern travel sections brought the first tourists since the American Revolution. Today there are 38 Americans, 2 Canadians and 15 Dutch homeowners. Island Estates, the original company that laid out the lots in the 1950s, has sold 100 with 125 more available.

The company has just completed a half mile of paved road between the wooded hillside and the beach.

The overall cost of living is about $500 US per month, up or down according to the couple. This includes a part-time maid and gardener, and entertaining once or twice a month such as a bridge party. The cost of living is considerably lower than on St Maarten. There are no land taxes but there is a transfer tax each time land is purchased. (See Chapter Ten for specifics.)

The island has direct dial telephone links with the world; 42 inches of rain; three expatriate car dealers with cars in stock; an Historical Society that lives as though Santa Claus stops every day.

The Dutch developed a second group of three islands as far away as they could get, thirty to forty miles off the coast of Venezuela. The ABCs – Aruba, Bonaire, Curaçao – are physically about as different as they could be. Like the US Virgins, these offer the same environment but in three descending population densities. CURAÇAO, 180 square miles, is most densely populated with 159 000. BONAIRE, 111.9 square miles, with the smallest population, 9000. ARUBA is the compromise island with 69.9 square miles and 64 000 people.

The three are out of the hurricane lanes. They receive about 23″ of rain and have ground like cement, so hard that gardeners buy soil from Venezuela. Schools are excellent. People speak – really speak – four languages, not counting the made-up Papiamento local tongue. Overall, the standard of living is high, but so is the cost, next only to Puerto Rico and the US Virgins.

Island ambience

The ABCs did not come into Caribbean prominence until 1914 when oil was discovered in Venezuela. Lying on the trade route, they grew commercially, especially Curaçao with oil, beer, soap, light industry and cruise ships. Aruba has light industry and oil, which is at the end of the island, out of sight. Aruba is less commercial. Bonaire is not commercial. If you are a spiritual descendent of Thoreau, pack your bag: a huge area is allocated to bird protection. Traffic goes through Curaçao. The ferry costs $70 for the round trip. There are no direct flights. It is rich in the priceless treasures of space, quiet and tranquillity. Like 'little sister' islands, one shops by phone to Curaçao. It has the small island disadvantages: coming and going are dependent on Curaçao, like St John to St Thomas, Virgin Gorda to Tortola,

Nevis to St Kitts. Imports come through Curaçao. It lacks those amenities which require minimum population.

As with all Dutch islands, they are genuine freeports without customs houses. This tends to attract a forceful type of young 'smarts'. Aruba has been especially heavily into smuggling Colombian coffee and drugs.

Their long dormant period in the eighteenth and nineteenth centuries leaves them without any residuals of the romantic past that are evident, and decorative, on other islands which flourished in the sugar, cotton and naval battles era. Consequently there is a *nouveau riche* feeling.

There is a strong casino crowd. Add to this the superb water life on all three islands, diving, snorkelling, surfing and boating, with enlightened governmental protection of the marine life and you get a sense of contemporary, outdoor, active gusto.

The Dutch keep a tight rein. They state bluntly that you cannot just arrive and expect to be sold a piece of land. They enforce strict landholder licensing, no work permits and income tax more severe than in most islands. The rate is low compared to the US but nevertheless to be considered. (See Chapter Ten.)

When you estimate building costs, keep in mind importing from Venezuela – duty free. Furthermore, you can do the buying and transporting yourself. Recently the six Dutch islands discussed whether to remain with Holland or go for complete independence. Five elected to remain with the Dutch: the Netherlands pours fortunes into them. Aruba, under Betico Cruz, elected for a ten year trial of independence with option to return. Observers note that Mr Cruz is friendly with Castro and was friendly with Bishop of Grenada.

At the time of writing, this situation is not fully crystallised. For buffs of history-in-the-making, it could be worth a bet.

Now we hop back to St Martin.

The French side comes under the jurisdiction of Guadeloupe, a department of France. If you live on St Martin you wander from the Dutch to the French, from the bustling to the quaint, under two flags yet daily ignoring both. Of course you shop on St Maarten and take it across the line. Technically it's smuggling. Continental expatriates tend to titter when confronted with smuggling, like women when they see a naked man. They know it's there but they snicker anyway. It's not an issue. The question is: do you want to live out and go downtown on weekdays, or live in the city centre and go out at weekends? St Martin does it both ways. The French side, however, grinds its legalities through Guadeloupe several islands distant.

One of the islands between St Martin and Guadeloupe, St Barts, is also French. The island was Swedish but was ceded to France with the plebiscite agreement that it could return to Sweden by simple plebiscite if the French did anything it did not like. It pays absolutely no taxes. It has always been known as a smuggler's heaven. It used to be cheap, but recently it has become expensive. Several excessively wealthy land-holders have a hard-to-define influence over the island. Retirement here would require unusual investigation.

Sandwiched between the French islands are five British islands: Antigua, Barbuda, St Kitts, Nevis and Montserrat. This is why living in the Caribbean always has a touch of holiday. You may have breakfast in a Dutch atmosphere, lunch in a British one and dinner in a French one.

ANTIGUA is at the hub, with direct flights to Great Britain and Europe, rather as San Juan is to north America.

English people have been retiring here for generations. Since the first settlers arrived in 1632, Antigua has been a hub of naval power. It is still a yachting centre. A person would be happier if he loved boats, as well as cricket and soccer. But land is hard to find. No beach front is available. Although Antigua is small and superficially romantic with its forts and anchorages, in the matter of development, it already has diversity. Facilities such as the hospital and district clinic are good. They serve as support systems for the nearby islands. As for the ambience in general, you might test your future social acceptability by inquiring about membership in the Mill Reef Club. Be sure to check your grandparents' credentials.

BARBUDA, 32 miles north of Antigua, is a dependency. Like all small dependencies, it periodically claims deprivation. Barbuda is flat, devoid of stream or spring. Its 75 square miles are not yet prepared to provide the amenities most retirees require. Surrounded by coral reefs, it is a gorgeous playground for snorkellers. At present it is suitable for part-time holiday investment. You can easily reach it for personal research via scheduled pleasure cruises from Antigua.

Forty-five miles west of Antigua are two plums ripe for picking: ST KITTS and NEVIS.

If any island has rivalled Antigua as a bastion of British might, it is St Kitts. Whatever residue from history you feel is proudly British. Yet the island has not been glamorised. The centre of the island is an extinct volcano with a 700 foot deep crater. The rest of the island, seen as a place to reside, is miles and miles of cane fields. The government is aiming at diversity. St Kitts is a stable little country with ample piped water, good roads, a healthy climate and the impression of steady, level-headed growth. The southern end forms a sort of tail where yachting becomes prominent, with the Caribbean glamour that accompanies it.

Holiday investment

The two to three hundred expatriates who own homes are equally divided among American, British and Canadians. Land is available. You can rent either furnished houses or apartments. (Cost details in Chapter Ten.)

You might start your investigation with Frigate Bay, on the southern 'tail'. It has a dramatic view of the sea and a good harbour. Land is available, from private owners as well as the Frigate Bay Development Corporation, which exposed all costs in a manner that could help you make further comparisons. For example, the Corporation explains such costs as EC $2000 sewerage connection fee and EC $300 survey fee; a stamp duty of 2% purchase price; assurance fund 0.2% purchase price; registration fee EC $7.20 and legal fee 2% purchase price.

NEVIS is an associated state with St Kitts in the British Commonwealth. Being only three miles south, with no more than twelve miles between their capitals, Nevis from the settler point of view is the same island. Both ferry and airbus link the two towns. Yet, the feel of Nevis is more urbane.

Holiday investment

In the time of Lord Nelson, Nevis was a refined outpost of British privilege. It still has a flavour that makes visitors feel gentle toward it. Its guest houses have a genteel atmosphere. Its 36 square miles and 13 000 inhabitants are well sprinkled with expatriates from Britain, Canada and the US. The slopes with the dead volcano at their centre are mildly forested, its beaches palm lined. Tourism is not dominant. Were Nevis not in the shadow of St Kitts it would undoubtedly be more noticeable as a prime small island for tranquil living. In the 1960s and early 70s its development was retarded by an unfavourable government on St Kitts, from which Anguilla successfully seceded. The relationship is now better and the present administration is thought highly of.

MONTSERRAT, 27 miles from Antigua, is the fifth member of this British cluster. To experience living here, think of these islands as exurbia surrounding a central city. That's the way retirees come to think of them, not as scattered little countries.

Montserrat is a well administered community. The cost of living is given in Chapter Ten. About half the 250 expatriates who own houses live here half the year or more. Americans comprise 40%, British and Canadians 30% each of the population. Most maintain cars and devote considerable time to gardening. For those a little nervous about leaving home, Montserrat is a soothing investment. There are three primary real estate companies. Report has it that the top people in all three are the same and that if one looks far enough into the books one will find the Colonial Development Company which is said to hold royal money.

Montserrat, like Anguilla, chose to remain a British colony rather than to opt for independence.

The island has good medical facilities, ample land with some beach front. The black sand beaches are hotter than white, a feature some home owners consider a control against undesirable beach crowding. Montserrat imposes a tax of 20% site value, 5% market value on land and house, 15% agricultural value. The tax is more complicated but this serves as an alert.

A hint of the cultural level is heard in the radio programming, produced in four languages and reaching as far as the US Virgins. Sometimes one can even find classical music: at the moment *Rose Marie* is coming through in French.

Farther south is another group of five British affiliated islands. But, typical of the Caribbean pattern, we have to go through France again.

GUADELOUPE, with its several small island dependencies, is the administrative centre for France in the Caribbean. If you were to live on St Barts or French St Martin your governmental matters would go through Guadeloupe. For everything else, Guadeloupe may provide an occasional evening of *Je ne sais quoi*.

Let us move on to that next group of five British islands.

DOMINICA was French until 1814 so it is no surprise that many of the people still speak a French patois, though English is the language of the island. The trouble with writing about these eastern Caribbean islands is – if I'm not on the island I love, I love the island I'm on. Right now, we're on Dominica.

This spectacularly lush, craggy mountain seems to dare you to tame it. Here the Caribes retreated to hold out until their demise. It has more water than it needs, more flowers, more trees, more waterfalls – and only 80 000 people for the 305 square miles. I would like to say it is dull, theft-ridden, a nauseating place to live so that no more outsiders would seek to spoil it. But it isn't any of those things. I could drop it from the text but the publisher would catch the omission. So . . .

About two hundred and fifty expatriates own homes: 100 British, 65 Americans, 20 Canadians and 65 various Europeans. About 30% of these stay all year round. (See Chapter Ten for the *Cost of Living*.)

In a later chapter is a statement by the Prime Minister regarding the island's attitude toward future home seekers. You can write for 'Policy Statement on the Holding of Lands by Aliens and Non-Dominicans'. It politely explains why the island must protect its inexperienced citizens from their own naiveté.

However, lest this approach seems to belittle the standard of living for continentals, we should recall the market in Roseau is so well provisioned, especially with excellent meats, that a surprised Texan reluctantly conceded it was 'as good as we have at home!' The local Tourist Bureau seems best equipped to answer questions about potential retirement. Write to: Dominica Tourist Board, Box 73 Roseau, Commonwealth of Dominica, WI.

You might reasonably assume we would go straight from Dominica to the other four islands of this British area but this is the Caribbean. You must go to France again, Martinique, a department of France proper, lies between Dominica and St Lucia, St Vincent, Grenada and Barbados.

BARBADOS, like Antigua, is the hub, the administrative centre for the UK in this part of the Caribbean. Barbados is not notably a yachtsman's dream like the rest of the West Indies. It is 100 miles upwind from St Vincent and no good gunkholing when you're there.

For those of you who have had enough adjusting and would like a loving climate with all comforts, Barbados is fully equipped: excellent hospitals staffed from the US and the UK, internal services fully established, even to internal telephoning free, and a pure-bred atmosphere: British and never anything but British.

Island ambience

So many expatriates live on Barbados that it is difficult to get a true count, for when does an expatriate become a long-time permanent resident? A good guess is 6000, spread equally among Americans, British and Canadians. Unlike the other islands, the majority do live here all year around, another factor increasing the sense of comfortable settledness. They maintain cars. Many have two cars. (See *Cost of Living* in Chapter Ten.)

Population is dense, about half a million on 166 square miles. Work permits are granted only for special expertise. Land is available to the extent that, at time of writing (1984) there is a buyer's market.

The hint of a class structure in the social environment takes time to evaluate clearly. The west coast is where the rich and celebrated have homes in a tight band along the beach, well hidden from the road by landscaping. Several families are 'old'. One patriarch described the relationship of his stratum with the masses, 'We do business with them but we do not roost with them.' It may take a while to learn just where you would roost. Descendants of the Welsh slaves, called redlegs, after three centuries still do not roost well.

However, if you fit, Barbados has been fêted for its healthiness since early colonial days. Of course, that too is a personal factor. George Washington's brother went to Barbados to cure a lung ailment. George visited his brother and contracted smallpox.

ST LUCIA is next, twenty miles south of Martinique. Much of its existence has been under French dominance. French patois is extensive, especially among the poor. The environment of St Lucia as a place to live is an undertone of British stability with an overtone of French playfulness. It is at once mellow yet emergent. It provides the amenities of a larger island yet is rich with forest and mountain. Land is available. In the ten years before 1983, 372 expatriates moved to St Lucia in the ratio of 3 Canadians, 6 Americans, 9 British. In the typical expatriate pattern, about 50% make their home here all year round. (See *Cost of Living*, Chapter Ten.)

ST VINCENT lies thirty miles south of St Lucia with this time no French, Dutch or Spanish between – just flying fish. Topographically St Vincent continues the theatrical beauty that starts with Dominica – forested mountain slopes peaking to a volcano. St Vincent is predominantly rural with dramatically fertile valleys abundant in fruits, vegetables and spices. It is less densely populated for its size, 100 000 on 150 square miles. St Vincent owns most of the uniquely attractive Grenadines. The flow of foreign settlers is towards these small dependencies between St Vincent, the mother island, and Grenada. In the last ten years the Grenadines have added amenities of such quality and in such quantity that it can only be explained by the conviction that mother has been pushing her chicks.

Island ambience

Expatriates in the St Vincent domain are about 30% Canadians, 30% Britains, 20% Americans and 20% mainly French, German and other Europeans. The income tax assessment on property is a complicated tax but the same as for locals, therefore it is (1) fair (2) low by expatriate measure. St Vincent gives the impression of not rushing to grab tourists but quietly attracting settlers to its dependencies. If true, the policy is smart. Retirees bring capital into the country, take none out. Once they make their initial large contribution through house and vehicle purchase, they feed a steady flow of cash into the public services, local shops and government fees. They ask little in return, and are no drain on schools or police. Probably the worst fault of retirees is that their inevitable greater affluence over most locals gradually creates a have and have-not division in the population which opportunists manage to convert to black and white division for the purpose of political mischief. By attracting retirees to its Grenadine dependencies, St Vincent takes advantage of a natural separation, and enjoys a new source of income from areas until recently of no economic value, while giving the main island time to raise the standard of living without social stress.

Local labour is plentiful, described by developer, John Caldwell, as 'easy to work with'. In ten years the growth of inter-island communications has been nothing short of eyebrow raising: there are inter-island flights to St Vincent mainland and Barbados; a daily service to Union from Grenada, St Vincent, St Lucia, Martinique and Barbados. This takes care of emergencies and brings every island into quick contact with the many hospitals and clinics available to all; it provides dock delivery of groceries and makes shopping under the various national banners a year-long fiesta. The Grenadines seem to have been created for playing hopscotch by boat.

Starting with St Vincent, and going down the Grenadines sounds like a conductor on a commuter train: Bequia 9 miles, Mustique 18,

Canouan 25, Mayreau 37, Palm 40, Union 41.

BEQUIA is the largest with 4422 acres, long a yachtsman's pet. It has now grown, with new shops, restaurants, bars, enlarged hotels, and is rumoured to be in line for an airstrip. Here's the safeguard for these islands – with only 4400 acres and lots of coastline, it can never become urban sprawl.

MUSTIQUE's retiree potential is not clear. Large and dominant local family control over much of the land clouds the future course of development. Also some very high society, jet-set ownership is not a factor most retirees would be comfortable with in their $60 000 to $150 000 homes. If tempted by this unusually beautiful little spot, which does have an air connection, you might get in touch with the Government Information Division of the Prime Minister's Office, Kingstown. At the time of going to press it is headed by an agreeable gentleman, Mr Leon Huggins.

CANOUAN has 1694 acres, almost all being handled by the Development Corporation which can be reached at Kingstown, St Vincent's capital. The island has a good harbour, an airstrip and tremendous potential for residences but at present the only shops and homes are spread around as though a village had not yet coagulated.

MAYREAU is owned by one family in St Vincent, a condition that augurs problems in real estate. A small hotel development in Saltwhistle Bay could provide comfort while you look around. The personnel is typically Caribbean: Tom Potter is Canadian, Undina, his wife is German.

PALM is privately owned on a 99 year lease by John and Mary Caldwell, from whom all information is available. Their address is: Palm Island, St Vincent, WI. This miniscule spot of about 130 acres is a unique venture. The entire island is surrounded by five beaches and a huge reef. It has been surveyed for 90 residences except in one area where there is a commissary, a beach club (the telephone available to homeowners), a construction firm, the beginnings of a marina and the beginnings of miscellaneous additional dreams. Twenty-three expatriates own homes and many more have land on hold. All plots are beach front. In effect it is a super idyllic suburb utilising the urban facilities of much larger Union Island, a mile away and reached by the developement's own private ferry. Palm is the geographic centre of the Grenadines as well as the prototype and standard bearer of man's enhancement of Nature's best. (See *Cost of Living*, Chapter 10.)

UNION is 2600 acres, next in size to Bequia and the end of

St Vincent. The government seems to be making Union into a mini-hub. Ten years ago I thought it the drabbest little nothing in the chain. Today it has a handful of retirees, two villages, a new government staff, new shops, new homes for locals and a movie-cum-discotheque. It is the airport and central city for Palm, Mayreau and Canouan. Land is available.

The next country as we travel south is GRENADA with the last and largest of the Grenadines, CARRIACOU. She hasn't been her old self recently but she's coming along nicely now. Among Caribbean *aficionados* Grenada and St Thomas are considered the two most beautiful works of Nature. That does not include what man has done.

Grenada had, and still has, what seekers could well vote the complete qualifications for heaven on earth: beauty, fertility, climate, water, yachting and some of the most easy-going, sweetest dispositioned people ever — all in the EC zone.

The question remaining is how safe is Grenada from another attempted take-over? It was never more secure. Finally, Americans west of the Mississippi know where the Caribbean is. The *Affaire Grenada* made it clear that other countries, Syria, Lybia, Algeria, Iraq, Russia, for example, which contributed millions to the proposed 'tourist' airport, realise the Caribbean is the soft under-belly of North America.

Since the First World War, Britain has withdrawn from the Caribbean gradually. The US seemed content to let her kids play in someone else's back garden. Most islands have thought of Canada as the only grown-up they could turn to. From Anguilla to Grenada you hear, 'Canada gave us this hospital – or school – or X-ray machine.' During the Depression, when Britain seemed to lose interest and the US never had any, Canada funded hospitals and schools, offered loans for public causes and sent gifts 'from the people of Canada'. Economically it was a good move. Canadians didn't lose. The West Indies were and are grateful. Even though the British Virgins are only eight miles from the USVI, subscriptions to *Time, Newsweek* and the *Reader's Digest* are filled by Canadian issues.

During the Grenada rescue expedition, mainlanders asked residents in the Caribbean whether they weren't afraid of the Russians. To answer bluntly but honestly, in full-scale war nobody is going to waste A-bombs on dinky little islands. The Caribbean would be safer than the mainland. As for more little infiltrations, North Americans are either alerted now or it won't matter.

People who know the islands are already now at work investing in Grenada. While we wait, let me share a memory of Grenada as she was and no doubt will be.

In 1970 some of us from the charter boat, *Maverick*, were roaming the magnificent fort that overlooks St Georges harbour. No unfriendly signs said 'keep out' so we entered a tunnel entrance. It went down, around and around into the depths of the fort. We wandered through a series of dark, cobwebbed rooms with only gun slots for light. The gallery ended abruptly. Nothing was on the stone wall in front but a rusty iron ladder leading up to a trap door. It was such a long, dirty way back that everybody voted me to climb the ladder. The trap door rose squeakily. I came face to knees with three policemen. In only gleaming white singlets and underpants, they slapped dominoes on to a box. Their eyes scarcely flickered towards me. I stared, not knowing whether to go up or down. The seconds piled up as the dominoes slapped. One of the men, without moving an eye, said quietly, 'You want your bread and water, I presume?'

Ten years later, I urged another group of boaters to repeat the fun. We approached the road up to the fort. It was blocked by a chain. A young soldier held a gun. I did not understand what he said so I pushed on. I understood the rifle pushed at my chest.

Now we can go back to collect our bread and water, happily. You can confidently, any time, put Grenada on your list to explore.

After Grenada, we are down where we started the chain, at TRINIDAD and TOBAGO.

Trinidad is wealthy with oil, pitch and fertile soil producing many fruits and grains. It has mountains, plains and water. But nothing describes Trinidad as a place to live except a picture book. It has had for years a large continental population, English, Spanish, French, Dutch, Portuguese, East Indian, slave and free Africans, Chinese. However, the bulk population is West Indian, often called blacks by the Indians, though most are not as dark, though not as fair as the Chinese whom the West Indians call whites, especially when they are envious because so many Chinese are high in government and commerce.

You see, Trinidad is a world unto itself. Even its terms have meaning only in Trinidad. The wearied cliché about its being a state of mind really does apply. Do you like parades? Parties about parades? Much of the nature of Trinidad is fun in the streets. Of course you could avoid it but if so, why move to Trinidad with its million and a third population? Carnival obsesses the mind for over a week. Partying occupies several weeks before. The echo of new calypsoes goes on long after. It seems silly to the northern mind but maybe warm weather in winter makes people playful. There are New Orleans and Rio. If you don't think it is joy, it is an annual damned nuisance.

On a high ridge above bubbling, busting Port of Spain, I spent some days at a monastery, an old-fashioned place complete with bells, benches and monks. You would never know Port of Spain existed. I could see the vast lowlands and rice fields to the south, and small villages looking unfinished. But no matter where you lived, you would probably go through Port of Spain frequently. As a city it might compare with Cairo for its energy to survive. In Cairo two taxi drivers will pull a customer as though to split him. In Port of Spain little boys watch until a tourist looks at a map or slip of paper, and then politely ask if they may help. Learning where the tourist wants to go, they walk in front to the destination then demand pay for guide service.

Outside the city the expected does not begin. You come upon a Hindu temple. A hop away you find a mosque. Around the Savanah at the city's centre, one feels as though on a Hollywood set: a perfect Victorian mansion stands beside a red and white stone striped Moroccan palace. Each contributing nation carries on its individuality without concession. How West Indian! How Caribbean! How Trinidadian!

Trinidad is the richest West Indian island. Its people have flair. Tourism is a poor third national industry. Country and city are comparatively large. Land is for sale where the agent finds it. Life is a *mélange* of peoples as on other islands, yet somewhat like living in a box of confetti. Consider this summary by the wife of a British Trade Commissioner who can describe seriously life in New Zealand or Winnipeg, or Montreal but when it comes to her twelve years in Trinidad, she giggles.

'Trinidad? Oh dear! I had twelve servants. I needed them all to get one day's work. But I loved them. I loved them all.'

Now TOBAGO is where you would go if you wanted something opposite from Trinidad. Tobago is larger than St Kitts, larger than Bonaire, than St Martin, but it feels small. It has deeply sculptured coasts with many harbours. Deep, short valleys with streams corrugate the central ridge from top to sea. The windward side has up to 100 inches of rain but the flatter leeward side has 60.

It is sparsely settled with 50 000 on 116 square miles, compared, for example, to Grenada's 110 000 on 120 square miles.

The topography, with many separate vistas, and the scarcity of people are part of why the island feels small, undisturbed, quiet. It feels like a good place for writers or other such misanthropes.

Tobago is 21 miles from Trinidad, a quick hop for provisioning and service, if you do not count waiting time for the inter-island planes. *Habitués* carry something to read.

It is fitting that the end of our island-hopping be Trinidad and Tobago – two such dissimilar islands so close in the same country! They have more mixtures of people, more pageants at religious festivals, more customs, and cuisines than others. Trinidad and Tobago is a condensed Caribbean.

How can one write of such a patchwork quilt as the Caribbean? Each patch a joy unto itself, yet a swatch of damask, woven to a square of linen, stitched to a snippet of ribbon. How many fingers have sewn those shores together? How much loving, how much sickness, what depth of tears has each absorbed? These memories are the soul of the West Indies.

Could you have a more exciting start for a new life than you have now – to choose among this galaxy which isle shall be the cradle of your tomorrow!

THREE
How to choose your island

Don't.

Let the island choose you. All have sand, surf and sunshine. All have differences, some obvious, some subtle. All are welcoming. There is only one you, retiree or pre-retiree.

The *alcaldes* of Culebra and Vieques, off-shore islands of Puerto Rico, called retirees a 'Non-Polluting Industry' worth cultivating. They bring in large sums for their homes. Thereafter, they keep a steady flow of cash going into local shops. They ask to take no money out. They bring experience to local business and volunteer for cultural activities. They don't strain the schools, and make few demands on the police. They are quiet, high quality residents. As a pre-retiree you may look on yourself as a future asset. Of course, as a foreigner, you may look on yourself as a possible disruption – just to keep your ego humble.

The island you eventually choose should measure up to *your* **Hopetos**, *your* **Never-agains**. Many retirees are remaining with their choice for the rest of their lives. Others keep moving, moving – an expensive way of finding what they want. And yet, to adapt the voice of Aldous Huxley, 'The Choice Is Always *Yours*'.

Probably the most prevalent cause of mistaken choice is palm tree fever. It's a form of love at first sight. The symptoms are loss of common sense and unwillingness to hear anything negative about 'your' island.

To ignore the true traits of an island is unfair to the place, unfair to yourself. Paradise it may be – and it may not be. When hotels tout their environment as Paradise, they advertise truthfully. If you can afford $60.00, or $100.00, or $280.00 a day, what the hotels provide in the setting created by Nature is as close to Paradise as you can get without dying first – as long as your money holds out. What retirees get, goes on as long as they do.

Paradise is part fiction, part self-delusion, the broth in which palm tree fever germinates.

The antidote is to keep your mind on yourself. Before looking for an island to retire on, be truthful with yourself about what kind of retirement you are looking for.

One island does not fit all tastes.

Which type of RETIREMENT is for you?

1 IMMEDIATE cutting of all roots

For dramatic impact, this is the greatest. You wake up the first morning on the island and – it's real! I'm still in my new life. How could I be this smart?

About the only decision you have to make immediately is over the furniture. Do you store it while you rent, or bring it with you? In the Caribbean rentals and sales almost always come furnished. Virtually everybody wants to move into a basic set-up, then send for favourite pieces later. If you expect to rent for some time and are sure you want your furniture with you, you may persuade the owner to remove his by signing a long enough lease.

2 GRADUAL turning over your business to others

You might be wise to add many more trips back than you wish to admit. A large portion of this arrangement seems to be fated for trouble 'back home'. The sweet adventure of sailing off into the blue frequently becomes overcast with the cloud of human frailty. This cloud does include 'really quite competent sons'. It's better not to tie yourself down with too many details at first. An apartment or a delayed-completion house leaves one more time to tend to the few unsevered roots.

Building a new house takes two years of your full attention. No matter what the completion date, enough nitty gritties will remain to occupy you for two years.

3 SPLIT YEAR: part-Caribbean; part-elsewhere

For part of the year will your house stand untenanted? Happily, housebreaking is not a worry except on a few islands, mostly the large ones. Your big concern is mildew and insects. As with all considerations, they are most easily settled during construction. The earth all around the outside can be treated before landscaping to retard tunnel termites (ground ants). These voracious creatures are attracted by pasteboard and books. They have the amazing ability to detect these delicacies from up to thirty feet away. Don't pack your absentee things in cardboard boxes near any little opening. The high ventilators, for example, or the west wall clerestory, are safer with hardware cloth over the screening if the house will be untenanted for long. It keeps mice out. If you hope for house-sitters with any regularity, a little anticipation of their needs will smooth your long-term relations. Make an area that can be designated as 'especially for you': a simple little desk, an empty book case, a few shelves in the work area for their hobby stuff. These are worth their cost in preserving your own privacy. For sitters, contact colleges for people on sabbaticals, and marinas for working couples living on board a boat.

Your basic decision is: do you want to manage two full-sized houses, or one plus a hideaway, or do you want to anticipate that each year you will want to stay longer in the Caribbean? (It gets to you!) So – if you think a hideaway for the winter months will do, keep in mind the idea of planning something larger than you will start out with. Design your hideaway to be easily expanded, when you finally decide to sell the old place.

4 INVESTMENT for renting until you go full time

This obvious daydream is enjoying rapid popularity.

Here is the combined advice of some real estate people. Small is easier to rent. You can reasonably rent two bedrooms and make a profit. You cannot, however, increase the rent enough to compensate fully for the cost of a third bedroom.

Location: you have a better chance of renting if your place is managed than if you try to handle it as a one-person agent. Think thoroughly around all the corners. Will you be dependent on the rent or will a tax deduction be enough? Renting for three or four weeks a year is not profitable. Furthermore, those long periods of vacancy are harder on a house in the Caribbean climate. If you buy or build where your house can be maid-serviced now (essential), will that location be where you will want to begin your great romantic retirement in five or however many years?

Real estate people say invest to make as much money as you can and take full depreciation. Buy where you can sell easily. Buy where the amenities appeal to two-weekers – not to retirees. Buy something small, fully outfitted with expendable furnishings. If you build, design it to look as West Indian as a daydream. Inside keep it bland and familiar. People on holiday do not want to vacuum, nor to be careful about anything.

They advise you to take the profit and island hop on your holiday, then invest whatever is over to offset inflation until you are ready to cut out completely.

They say that to mix renting and personal holidays results in not enough of either. Ask a couple who do visit their own place between rentals how they liked their holiday. If they tell the truth it will most often be, 'We worked like hell the whole damned time!'

If you are choosing an island for rental, study the rental business (not under a palm tree on a beach). What will it be like five years from now? What are the dependable signs for an appreciation of your investment – paved roads coming (whose money?), condos coming, shopping centre coming, casino coming? Does its future harmonise with what you have in mind for yourselves? A flower-draped cottage with lots of hammocks for the family get-togethers? If so, better check that casino bit again. According to taxi drivers, when Sint Maarten put in a row of casinos the cost of bread rose three times in one year. A good investment, maybe, but is it where you want to live? Maybe you should check out a small island a few minutes' ferry ride away and mark it for retirement when you sell the investment.

5   RENT until you are sure of yourselves, and of your island

The voice of experience recommends it. It does take emotional control. If you rent in the style you hope to maintain, you'll watch your capital shrink. However, there are sweet little West Indian places, beach cottages on little islands. There you can hide away and watch, and find out what it is like to soak in leisure. You may be incompatible. That would be a crucial discovery. Facing full retirement can be a trauma, even under a coconut tree – but that's not likely. There will be too much going on.

A series of six-month rentals can give you basic understanding that in the long run may save you a bundle.

You can start with either two of opposing attitudes: find the island you think you can love forever – go out to others on short visits and, maybe, confirm your judgement. Or, you can deliberately start out with a couple of islands you think you will not like for long. Maybe you'll be surprised yourself. Either way, this can be a time of exploration and growth such as you've not known since your first Scouting hike.

For your furniture, there is now an obvious solution coming into favour – the construction of a 'grandma room' at the back of a relative's house, or it could be the enclosing of a back porch, or the finishing of an attic. The cost of the room is reduced by the cost of a year or two of storage.

If you finally decide you do not want the furniture, your heirs inherit it early, or they sell. If you do want it, the relative gets an extra room. The fact is, when many people get their stored furniture back, after a couple of years living with the Caribbean's light, open, bright furnishings, their beloved old stuff suddenly looks as dull and hot and stodgy as the life they used to live.

So much for the different types of retirement; what about the different types of retirees to match?

What kind of RETIREE will you be?

1 VELVET COATED (or gowned) ROMANTIC EXPLORER

Do you see yourself, deep tanned, garbed in batik, strolling into the inn each evening for a planter's punch, first-naming the locals and long-nosing the tourists? These are numerous. They buy maintenance-free living and jet off somewhere during the summer months. If you see yourself as one of these, perhaps you would not want a house, even less a cottage. Check the maid and repair service early in your investigation of a dream island. Errol Flynn and Maureen O'Hara were never shown fixing a water pump or dashing to the third grocery shop because the first two are out of flour, meat and washing powder, and the island-wide shopping stampede is on.

2 DANIEL BOONE of the Grenadines?

If you are likely to be moving on every time ten people create a crowd, perhaps you ought not to buy a house. On the other hand, there are many, many islands where you can be alone, probably for years to come. The islands are developing so fast that it seems you hardly get adjusted to bare feet all day before they hang up a stop light. Yet this fast growth can occur only within the limits it sets itself. One couple, with a luxurious apartment in an affluent part of New York City, built what is virtually one large room with some visual room dividers. When they were gleefully told progress was at least reaching them – electricity had arrived – they wailed, 'But we love our Coleman lamps!' Their property is approachable only by small boat. They leave their tiny sloop at the marina during their absence.

A Daniel Boone shouldn't so much as look at a development. Quoting the ex-President of the Real Estate Association of the USVI, 'Most developments take five years to get started. After that, it's cement mixers for ten years.' If you really want solitude – or let us say last century innocence and calm – buy land from a native family, preferably approached from the water. Then you've got the West Indian McCoy. But squint when you look at that darling little island and visualise what a cruise ship could do to it. Try Barbados, Culebra, Tobago, Cannouan, Bonaire, Jost Van Dyke, Nevis.

3   A TRUE BOAT PERSON

First question: 'Is your partner one as well?' If you both are, enough said. That's perfect. The Caribbean always has been a yachtsman's world.

But, if only one of you genuinely loves the boat, usually the man, (although his lady is willing to 'pull a string' once in a while), that couple had better study the anchorage in relation to the house. It's not too bad if the boat can be anchored in view. He can emerge from the bilge once in a while and blow a greasy kiss. If he has to drive the length of the island to his boat, the marriage may soon feel the disruptive force of a triangle. It's an axiom, that if a marriage has a weak spot, the Caribbean will find it. One way is through a boat. The other is through low cost liquor.

4   MOTHER GOOSE type, always in need of people?

Perhaps for you the best starting places are some of the well-settled, expatriate enclaves such as northern St Lucia, several on St Croix, the north shore of Jamaica and Frigate Bay on St Kitts. For you the need is to cushion the change of environment with the comfort of familiar faces and talk. Then, if you find yourself drawn to the rural beauty of less populous areas, check the education level of the school system. Some islands have schooling for five or seven years, then the children have to go to another island for the higher grades. This puts a lid on the intellectual level of all those who cannot afford the boarding school fees. They may be bright and friendly, but in time you want to be able to make an allusion to John Barrymore without evoking a pause and, 'He the new man in legislature?' You can feel the level of schooling at the library, at any public entertainment, in radio programming. To evaluate the lack of schooling is not a disparagement; it merely facilitates some compensations on your part. The Dutch islands have the best educational level – the graduates must be able to *speak* four languages, five in the ABC's. The Dutch side of St Martin is compatible with gregariousness.

You'll find expatriates who are Rock Happy. They can sound downright desperate. Their extreme disillusionment may upset you, until you get the hang of it. It's not serious. Every person raised on a continent gets Rock Happy from time to time. Almost irrationally, they feel they will explode if they can't get to one really well stocked drapery shop; hear one really good live concert; get away from people who talk about nothing but scrubbing their eternally dirty boat bottoms.

As a potential retiree questioning expatriates, you will benefit by distinguishing genuine disillusionment from brief attacks of Rock Happiness. Retirees tend at first to go 'back' for three or four weeks. In the second or third year, they may still be going back for three or four weeks but return in two. It's strong medicine, this azure water and golden sunshine.

I was hit by Rock Happiness suddenly. I flew to San Juan and looked up the outbound planes. Should I go to Philadelphia – right away? Then I visualised the acres and acres of car tops around the airport and the interminable limousine ride past miles and miles of tiny shops, sited cheek to cheek.

How about New York? Then I recalled the smell of exhausts while waiting for the bus. Asphixiating!

I went to an early movie – and then caught the first plane back to St Thomas – cured.

Running away with Rock Happy blues produces a beneficial side-effect. When you return to your island, you have the feeling, oh, it's so good to be home! Your island becomes home. After a while you may turn to the neighbouring islands for a day of Rock Happy escape. The effect is the same as one of your former trips 'downtown'. You get a lot done and you're hot, tired and oh, so glad to be home. The large nearby islands can soon become your downtown and they have a big advantage over the old downtowns. You get to them over the same routes and through the same scenery that you fell in love with when you first saw the Caribbean.

When you can spend a day shopping, with lunch in such super little cities as Old San Juan, or Fort de France, or St George's and sum it up: 'It's exciting, all right, but I wouldn't want to live there,' while curling up cosily in your new hammock under your own mango tree – you've discovered **Your Island**.

It is true that some people retire to the Caribbean and never seem to learn anything from it except the price of rum and when the last plane leaves. An obvious vulnerability of condo owners.

Getting acquainted with the local people can open whole new pastures of calming thought. On Anguilla, for example, I rented a taxi from one of those incomparably charming older islanders whose speech and spirit seem to go back to Sir Walter Raleigh. The taxi had no spare wheel. When I looked at the bald tyres and the roads set with pointed things, like a fakir's bed, I wondered. Then I found the battery was weak and Charlie Gumbs had no spare. I said, 'Charlie! When you don't have something you absolutely can't do without, what do you do?'

Charlie studied the situation. 'When you do not have something you absolutely cannot do without . . . (long pause) . . . (inspired!) . . . you use something else.'

I have repeated that to myself many times in the past fifteen years. It is a life philosophy.

While you are testing islands, it is a time to test yourself. Would you still like to dress up once in a while? Then you might want to stay close to the southeast part of Sint Maarten; to Montego Bay, Jamaica; the Caymans; the heart of Port of Spain; the Condado of San Juan. If, however, you feel you have dressed up a thousand times too often, try a small house in the foot-hills of quiet Montserrat, or a cottage within easy distance of Nelson's Dockyard, Antigua. Rent a cottage for a month out of season on Grand Anse, Grenada. In such spots you should find the Caribbean has known about psychotherapy for hundreds of years.

Many Americans will not venture beyond the flag that shelters the US Virgins and Puerto Rico. These facts may be soothing: Montserrat, Anguilla and the British Virgins are, by the will of their inhabitants, under the direct control of England. As for stable St Lucia and the Dutch islands, Canadians have been well-established there for two generations. If in doubt, check the banks on any island. This does not mean that others are not stable or responsible. The above fact is for those who place an extra high priority on the protection from the flag.

In all of us our sense of elapsed time is influenced by the numbing effect of familiarity. Here's a device to help you measure the new against the old. When you are home, about to go shopping, start timing yourself – putting on your coat, maybe changing your dress and shoes, getting the car out of the garage or walking to the train, waiting for the commuter train, parking and walking to the shop. Then do it all in reverse, including the change back of clothes, timed.

Now do the same, this time in a Caribbean setting. Take an extreme opposite. You're on Palm with twenty other retirees. You are going shopping a mile away on Union Island. Start – just as you are, in slacks, halter, espadrilles. Pick up your purse. Don't lock the house. Walk quarter of a mile to the ferry boat. Jump aboard. Wait maybe ten minutes. Sun yourself. Read. Doze. The boat takes off one mile across the limpid waters of the Grenadines. There are tourists aboard ooh-ing and aah-ing. Let's say the ride takes eight minutes – it's a slow boat. You jump ashore at Union and walk through the three super-markets – a mile? Take the boat back. Realistically, the boat won't be ready to leave the moment you appear. You sit on the hotel verandah for twenty minutes; long enough for an ice. The boatman waves when he is ready. It takes eight minutes to get back; five minutes to your house. You don't have to change your clothes.

Compare the two. It might just be that you would take less time by island-hopping than by driving downtown.

Compare the pleasantness.

Here's a true case: a man with a broken neck received all the treat-ment Tortola hospital could give him. He was helicoptered from the hospital lawn to the Vet's Hospital on Puerto Rico in half the time he would have taken to go by ambulance from his suburban home through the traffic of a big city.

If you ever want more pinpoint information, write to the Govern-ment Chief Information Officer in the capital town. This will not be the exact title for all islands, but it will be close enough to start a correspondence. Tourist Boards do not have this kind of information. Some of them do not answer. If nobody answers you, that tells you something about the island, too.

Here's another game to play to learn about your choice of sand and surf. Go to the hub island; Antigua, Puerto Rico, Trinidad, St Thomas, Sint Maarten, Martinique, whichever is yours. Chat with expatriates who live there. They'll enjoy talking about their choice so long as you don't mention 'back home', which they left.

Ask them why they live on the hub island rather than on your island.

When you get back to yours, ask the expats why they live there rather than on the livelier hub.

Islands have personalities and, like humans, they cannot be known really well on a short acquaintance. Let's take two which on the surface have nothing in common except uniqueness: Palm, which you may have an image of by now, and Saba, often called a collector's island because it is so utterly utter.

They have about the same number of expatriates owning houses – plus or minus twenty. Saba is actually a mountain peak, nothing else – no beach. Palm is a sand bar – all beach. Saba was among the earliest islands to be inhabited by the Dutch. Less than two decades ago Palm had nothing – not even one palm. (Its name was Prune!)

Until the last few decades, everything bound for Saba was sloshed through rough surf to a rock ledge by lighters from a ship lying out. People walked up 1300 feet on steps hand-cut into the mother rock.

When neighbouring islands around Saba began spreading airports, the Sabans decided it was time they had a road. They asked the government for help and waited to start until they would learn how much the government would contribute. Government engineers said a road was impossible: no contribution. The Sabans then said, 'Well, we don't have to wait any longer. We can start tomorrow.' The men built fifteen miles of road by hand. It took twelve years. Next, they wanted an airport.

The government said, 'On a mountainside? Impossible!'

For more than two decades planes have been landing on a tiny clearing the men made by knocking the top off a big hill. Dr Hartog, one of the Dutch island's own writers, described the planes landing 'like butterflies on a postage stamp'.

By the early 70s the Sabans hit their peak of ludicrousness; a deep water pier. They didn't even have a beach.

This time the government gave help.

Now to the sand bar, Palm, where John and Mary Caldwell landed, alone, less than two decades ago. It had five beaches separated by mosquito swamps, a little scrub and maybe a fish, or two thousand, on the reef which almost encloses the whole island. The neighbouring isles were just anchorages. There was no bank, no supermarket, no cinema, no clinic. Like their neighbours two hundred and fifty miles to the north, Mary and John built what they needed – a beach club, a tiny hotel, but of perfect West Indian design. Then, with untrained help from nearby islands, guest cottages sprouted, then homes for expatriates, a construction company, and an inter-island boat service to Union's new airport. By October 1983 John and his two sons had filled in the last of the swamps. Every mosquito got deportation papers. The latest news is that stateside engineers are investigating the possibility of a a yacht club, condominiums, more houses. 'The whole thing; a much bigger programme than the Beach Club,' says John, with a shrug. 'It's time.'

Of course it's time. They've been at it for seventeen years, seven days a week without a holiday. And people are always asking retirees, 'What do you DO all day?' Don't you agree it is high time the Caldwells produced something new – like a yacht club?

On both these dissimilar islands, the thing you absorb if you stay for a while is fervour. Commitment is their atmosphere. You can feel it in the new countries of the Near East and Africa. People have purpose and determination. After a week or so you feel like running back to pick up any day-dreams you discarded along your life.

How do you choose an island? Go slowly enough to see beyond the beach and the airport. They all have personalities.

One trait you can check on before you even head for the Caribbean is population density. This can be deceptive. The arithmetic needs investigation.

Here's the formula: square miles divided into population = people per square mile – population density.

Island	Sq. miles	Population	Density
Anguilla	35	5 000	143
Aruba	69.9	64 000	911
Barbados	166	254 000	1 530
Bonaire	111.9	9 000	80 +
Curaçao	180	159 000	883
Haiti	10 714	5 200 000	392
Montserrat	39.5	13 000	328
USVI	133	120 000	902

The figures are helpful, but require judgement. The ratio for the ABCs is accurate enough for a big decision: if you think yourself a spiritual descendant of Thoreau, the population density points to Bonaire with flamingoes for neighbours. If you prefer plenty of opportunity for take-off to the old world and modern amenities, it's Curaçao.

The US Virgins seem to have about the same number of people to the square mile as Aruba. Aruba is flat. St John and St Thomas are not. Aruba is one island. The Virgins are three. The whole centre of St John is park. These considerations prepare you to expect the feeling of crowdedness to be more apparent on St Thomas than on Aruba, despite the 902 versus 911.

Barbados is essentially flat. However, the population is concentrated on the southwest, south and southeast coasts. Living along the north you would have a local density of a less populated island, but the heavy concentration only a few miles away by car would mean more amenities close by for you, quick access to government facilities and probably a more tiring, less interesting weekly trip 'to town'.

People-per-square-mile is not a precise definitive trait of an island because it does not tell you the distribution of the people; are they massed in flatland villages as in Haiti, or spread about with no real village as on Virgin Gorda? The population/square mile is a better indication of certain living conditions – services which can be supported only by a minimum of inhabitants or explain an expensive utility rate such as electricity or telephone on a low population density island.

Following are basic figures, as in 1982, for your reference as you go. Happy island hopping!

Island	Square miles	Population
Anguilla	35	5000
Antigua	171	75 000
Aruba	70	64 000
Barbados	166	254 000
Bonaire	112	9000
Cayman	100	17 200
Curaçao	180	159 000
Dominica	305	80 000
Dominican Republic	19 120	4 300 000
Grenada	120	110 000
Guadeloupe	680	330 000
Haiti	10 714	5 200 000
Jamaica	4450	2 100 000
Martinique	425	325 000
Montserrat	39.5	13 000
Nevis	36	13 000
Puerto Rico	3435	3 400 000

Saba	5.0	1020
Statia	7.5	13 000
St Kitts	65	35 000
St Lucia	238	125 000
St Martin/Maarten	37	25 500
(both sides)		
St Vincent	150	110 000
Tobago	116	50 000
Trinidad	1864	1 300 000
British Virgin	59	12 000
Islands		
US Virgin Islands	133	120 000

FOUR
How to choose your site for home, rental or condo

To quote dozens of real estate salesmen, you will buy your land 'for the view. Everybody does.'

Every Caribbean island will provide you with hundreds of views. Beauty is everywhere. You will stand and drool over the site, every time you go near. Of course you should – it will be right off a calendar. After your fever subsides a little, you can do two things to restore your emotional balance; neither will diminish your view.

1   Go to some other gorgeous locations and pretend *they* are your choice. Stand and visualise on each that it has the view you will enjoy day after day, year after year. (It won't be too bad.)

2   Go back to the site you are seriously considering. Close your eyes and then turn to face the view. This will be your view while you

are washing dishes; asleep; in the bathroom; reading; hacking out a tree; fixing the septic line.

Of course you will buy 'your' view. But the little exercise above will strengthen your purpose to approach these other aspects of living on that superb piece of ground.

1 (Overwhelmingly No. 1) – The breeze

To do a thorough job of it, you need to visit the site at different times of day, preferably at different seasons, though this may not be feasible. Buy six Chinese anti-mosquito coils, the kind that are burned in most small inns and native homes. They are available at almost any general or hardware shop. Burn one coil in each corner of your site. Don't try to identify the direction of the wind by holding a cigarette. It does not burn long enough and your body diverts the current.

Note the entrance of the breeze from some far distant point carefully. It will be easterly. At other times of the year it may be more northerly or southerly. You can learn this from anyone who lives near.

2 Note – are you in the lee of a hill?

If so, the location may be windless. If so, it will at times be insect-ridden. However, a hill does not necessarily cut off the breeze. It may change its direction, as may a deep gully. This is why you should mark the direction of the wind across your whole plot, with a mosquito coil, not with a cigarette.

Incidentally, if your salesman discouraged you from going to so much trouble – 'I know the wind here!' – that's all the more reason for testing it yourself. After all, you are not putting him to any bother – unless you discover something he will not like.

3 Note – Is your site below the road?

If so, you save about 50% on material handling.

4 Note – Do you see where you can drain off rain water (grey water) some day from a paved street, or natural run-off?

A small grey water cistern for toilets and gardening gives your site a big plus on a dry island.

On our first big island-hop shopping trip we started at Gustavia, the harbour capital of St Barts. Its early years as Swedish still clung to the square stone houses but the language, the shrugs and haute cuisine were dramatically Gallic. Friends told us Gustavia was on the way to anywhere. There was St Maarten so clear in the background; Saba, Statia, St Kitts just a few miles away around us. We could reach them by little feeder planes, although we thought the small local boats more fun.

Street markets everywhere proved to be crowded spots at wide places in the road. We learned to prepare christophine and dashine, land crabs and — well, Fran's department. From island to island, the trading was easy; the money did the talking, with gestures. The women in the foreground hid from the camera lest it steal some of their soul. Usually they were boisterous, as curious about us as we about them.

Markets along a waterfront are especially fun, unpredictable. At St Thomas we came upon a load of coconuts from the Dominican Republic. You hold out your hand with 50¢ and the man lops the top off a nut for you. I held the nut aloft to pour a stream into my mouth — then I pretended I really did mean to cool my eyes, nose and neck!

For urgent shopping, such as a spool of thread or a new lid for our wok, we learned you can't beat the little hometown general store. My favourite is Penn's right on Main Street in central Road Town, Tortola. One never looks for anything. The clerk knows just where it is — behind something else, or upstairs, or over the house next door.

We soon agreed with old-timers that there is absolutely only one way to island-hop — by Inter-island Mail Boat. The money difference between inter-island boat and little plane isn't determinant. It's the fun of lolling on deck with chickens and goats an extra hour while grumbling about life always being sooooooo busy.

The newer inter-islanders tend to have metal hulls. However, wooden boats are still built under the trees on some small islands. Shipwrights continue their ancient skills. They can eye a length of timber, whack away with an adze without benefit of template and produce a waterproof fit. But it's a doomed art. Motor launches are in.

A most delightful bonus on the shop-hop was meeting Patty Heyliger. She was the cashier where I was able to buy razor blades but not a razor: 'Every man on Saba already has a razor.' Sixteen year old Patty had been sent to a Miss World contest on St Maarten by the Saba Ladies Organisation. St Maarten sent her back saying, 'Dress her as a queen.'

Well, why not? They're everywhere. They're intelligent. Their hourly rate is favourable, on St John or any other island. I've sat on my meditation bench thirty feet above my house, out of sight, and watched a family of goats race up to the garden entrance, wait while one went ahead and peered through the glass doors of the living room. There had to be an 'all clear' given because they all scampered down into the hibiscus together. They also all scampered out together under the shower of rocks.

Of all the traffic jams the most startling are Moko Jumbie walkers of Carnival. It happens at a different time on each island. Many are related to Easter. Banks and newspapers post dates of Carnival parades on their home island as well as on neighbouring islands.

Quite the opposite of downtown at Carnival are the little harbours where your inter-island launch pulls up to the jetty. Harbours provide a continuous treasury of old-time craft skills. If you drift into a shallow harbour like Bequia's or Anguilla's Road Harbour, you may see the mast of one boat block-and-tackled down to the deck of another in order to have bottom paint, without benefit of travel-lift and haul out.

Mayero (Mayreau) in the Grenadines is one of the least developed little islands. All the Grenadines are about this far apart, just a windsurfer hop if you're not carrying groceries. Union is the new hub island holding the future of neighbours such as Mayero.

On a truly unemerged island one never knows where one's next meal is coming from. Juli Soars of Anegada sometimes gets hers through a window from a passing fisherman. As in the Grenadines, the small British Virgins seem everywhere to live on the edge of the sea. Juli's restaurant, Neptune's Treasure, is no more than thirty feet from the water.

The strange truth about the Caribbean is that even the most densely populated islands, Barbados, for example, do provide an unrivalled calm, a West Indian softness of living, if you look for it. The northeast coast of Barbados is called Scot-land for its rugged beauty and sense of highland privacy. Through the glassless window of the Edgewater Hotel while you rest your shopper's feet you can let your soul search for greater harmony with the world as Nature meant you to know it. Yet in thirty minutes we were back in Bridgetown.

Even on densely populated, sophisticated Puerto Rico, only thirty miles from sprawling San Juan, rise twenty-five storey luxury condos. Sprouting from an immensity of flat land dotted with fishing villages that look like tropical fishing villages, Puerto Rico provides a nearly unique triple-level living: rural, super-urban and sky-borne all in one. This is the Fajardo area.

The hideaway homes of today's retirees are as different as their thousand daydreams. Here's a glimpse of one home that fascinates everyone. It embodies many basic Caribbean ideas, looking quite improbable yet being thoroughly solid. The short building on the left encompasses all bathroom functions, visually separated. The room on the right has all four walls louvered. It could be used in any way, or seasonally changed. The living-dining-kitchen area is in the two storey unit behind the bathing unit.

Now here is the genius of Caribbean life style. Everything is open to the air, the sun, the flowers, yet psychologically closed. The roof dips down protecting the room yet not encasing it as walls do. The kitchen, to the left, is sturdily enclosed against weather and intruders. Immediately beyond the great hall are the stairs, unroofed as is the Caribbean privilege and economy. The wall of lattice, difficult to see into, easy to see out of, creates the illusion of a wide niche. Here is a large bed, a comfy corner for napping.

All the photographs were taken by the author, Sydney Hunt, and are his copyright.

5   If your site belongs to a developer, expect development

There will be a rapid change after five years. Note the direction of major flow of traffic and village growth.

6   Read the weeds

If weeds are tall and thick, you have rainfall. Skinny weeds forecast skinny plants.

7   Take a soil sample

You gain only sorrow by hiding the truth from yourself. With the truth you can accomplish progress while you have workmen on the site. Send the sample to the nearby agricultural station. Stave off any attempt by the station to send a man back to look at your site. Say you would rather wait until the house is finished.

8   If you have a hillside, think about leaving the big rocks

With rocky hillside all around, if you smooth off your land, you will have a scab. Rocky gardens are dramatic and you can still get in a row or so of carrots.

9   You will change your site

The sites around you will be changed. What control is there? Has the developer firm plans or might he switch ideas if someone waves money at him? It has happened – oh merciful Lord, has it ever happened! Is the adjacent land government-owned or private? Is it for sale? Is there space between you and the view for a condominium? A restaurant – with a band? A marina – with power tools?

If you are tempted by a new condo: is there room for another hi-rise between you and the view? Will highway growth from airport to 'town' pass near? Will you be correctly oriented to the breeze? How frequent have the resales been? Rent for a week without revealing your interest in buying.

10   Visit your site at night and listen

Are you downwind from a band? They practise all week. Water makes sound travel. Windows are open day and night. How sensitive are you to barking dogs, crying children and reggae radio?

11 Is a large unpaved road passing near you?

Is it to be paved soon? Does a politician own it? A developer? This could be much in your favour, if you are looking for investment; or against you, if you are looking to escape from your urban past.

12 If you are near a beach

Walk to it at four o'clock in the afternoon, especially after a hot, dry day. Check the sandflies. The compromise to mull over is: closer to the beach, more sandflies, less view; higher up the hill, fewer bites, longer view.

13 If you have a boat

An off-shore is a plus feature for storm protection.

If you buy close to the water, to be near your boat, remember two things about a beach: 'He who builds on sand . . .', and, from 4 o'clock until dark during part of the year, sandflies are a possibility, though not a certainty.

Many successful structures have been built on beaches. Be sure to check the solidity of the foundations at high-water time and anticipate storm tides. Have the walls sunk deep enough. The wall foundations of Oranjested, lower town, Statia, have stood for two centuries.

Plan a wide paving around the house so that it can be sprayed if need be some months. The paving need not be expensive but keep in mind that unsupported flagstones will crack along the mortar.

14 Now

If you think you have evaluated a certain site maturely, you can do a quick, easy exercise to mark out the location of your house. Don't brush off this gimmick. Before you build you will have to locate and the way it is usually done on emergent islands is less accurate, more trouble and more costly.

Get six plastic knitting needles, a ball of string, a pocket knife or scissors, half a dozen paper clips, and a means of determining east. A scout's pocket compass is adequate. This small set of portable items can perform a very basic task. You may as well buy them before your trip.

Stand on your boundary facing the breeze, about halfway along the length of that line. Back off to the west (or opposite boundary) about where you would like the house. Push a needle into the ground. Cut a piece of string many feet longer than any side of your house will be. Wrap the middle of it around the needle and extend it in both directions, keeping it at right angles to the breeze (which is probably coming from the east). You will now have a north end and a south end. Tie the ends of the string to two more needles and stick them in the ground.

The open wall of your house should be built along this line. This is not necessarily the front of your house, nor the entrance, nor the deck. It is just the open-to-the-breeze side. It is the side which will make the indoors of your house as delightful as the Caribbean is outdoors – all year long.

You may move north or south along the line to change the position of your house within the plot, but do not change the right angle of your line in relation to the breeze.

Now, move back and forth along the line, hanging a paper clip, or any marker, where the outside limits of that wall will be. Cut two equal lengths of string which are a couple of yards longer than your house will be wide (or whatever you call the distance from the string to the opposite wall). Tie these two pieces of string where you have the two paper clips and walk away from the line of string extending the two lateral strings. Bring the far ends together. You will have formed an isosceles triangle. At the apex stick a needle into the ground.

Locate the midpoint between the two paper clips. Cut a piece of string to stretch from midpoint to apex. This line is at right angles to your open-to-the-breeze wall. It is also the centre line of your house. From the midpoint measure along the bisecting line until you have the depth you want for your house. Put a needle into the ground. Stretch some string of the same length as the opposite wall right and left, parallel to the breeze wall. Open your triangle sides and move them away from the apex till they mark the remaining two sides of your house. You now have a simple outline of your house, oriented to the breeze. Look at your view. The string marks your imagined walls.

Your contractor can build inside those strings. Your architect can design inside those strings. No matter what they do, you will have oriented your house to both breeze and view.

Better save this part of the book, if no other. You won't find the scheme anywhere else. I have seen local contractors get so fussed up

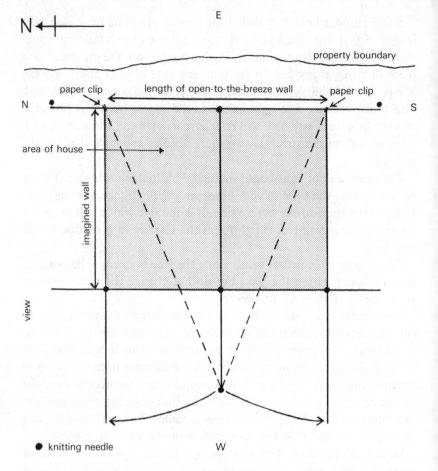

trying to lay out a house to the breeze that they have actually given up the job. One was one of my homes.

After you catch your breath, check out these items:

a) The cost of bringing in electricity to your site. Add 25% to a government estimate, 50% for estate agent's unless you know the answers intimately.

b) The cost of a generator as an alternative. You can find an expatriate with one if you look beyond the electric grid. Also, consider a wind generator.

c) Does the island have a petrol station, or will you have to buy gasoline by the drum?

d) Look into the possibilities of a gas stove for cooking. How reliable is the supply of propane?

e) A solar heater for water can be taken for granted.

f) Does the telephone wire use the same poles as the electricity? Put your name on the waiting list at the telephone company. There is no penalty if you back off.

g) Check the condition of the road. If it is not paved, find out who owns land between you and the end of the paved road. If it is a politician, give yourself A +. If several families own it, A, if natives, B, if one family, C. If the road is rough, make a mental note about more car repairs.

But perhaps you have already decided to go in for a condominium.

The risk in the Caribbean is the same and probably no more than with condominiums anywhere. You should get a local lawyer to read the contract. Also get him to check the land title – is it freehold or leasehold? The alien land-holder's licence – does each apartment owner have to apply for his own? This is a good question for you to discuss directly with a government official, the permanent secretary of the Ministry of Natural Resources, or whatever the variation on that theme is for that island.

If the condominium advertises 'air-conditioned', look it over carefully. It may not be oriented to the breeze. Many of them sell only the view because it is a fast sale. If the building is correctly oriented, air-conditioning may be included because so many mainlanders simply will not consider anything else. They cannot believe in the Caribbean air. I learned this while writing publicity material for a large hotel. The rooms on the west and south did need air-conditioning. The building was a huge cube. There was no way to avoid south and west rooms. On the north and east the rooms did not need it. Nevertheless, they were fitted with old units, many of which did not work. Some merely had instrument panels like stage settings. This was not a matter of deception. The management yielded to visitors at the front desk who would not go upstairs without an air-conditioner.

Also investigate the advertising claim, 'situated in the unspoiled serenity of . . . .'. Serenity was spoiled when the condominium was built. Evaluate how much serenity remains. Drop by at breakfast time and before dinner.

Check out the ownership of the land in front of the condominium. If it belongs to the same company, you may be able to get a clause permitting you to change suites if an additional building is put up in front. If it belongs to a different company, you have no control. In a

Check list of details hard to recall

Compare Three			
	1	**2**	**3**
Island			
Date visited			
Wind direction			
Lee of hill			
Cost of bring elec.			
Above/below road			
Grey water cistern			
Line of traffic			
Soil test			
Soil depth			
Rainfall: east or west end			
A development			
Noise upwind			
Paved road			
Beach sandflies			
Telephone poles			

year or so you may have as your romantic Caribbean view the parking spaces of a new condominium. It's happened.

All these tiny details! Some are caused by ignorance when entering a new area, some by the excitement of retirement and some by the blind love of an island. One couple recently completed a gorgeous $200 000 plus home but only after some months did they think of storm doors. Then they found that their excitingly curved windows and columned doors could not be fitted with hurricane shutters. They had forgotten them. So had their architect!

Try to stay in love with at least two islands until you have checked out the dull things such as rights of way, electricity, road paving – it will help you to stay on keel. It's all right to be in love with two girls up to the time you propose to one!

All these words of caution are certainly not meant to dampen your enthusiasm. They are to enhance your enjoyment – and make all your surprises happy ones.

Special for non-retiring investors

A condo has the greatest financial advantage — at first. Tax break. Less cash outlay. No headaches over management and service. The young buyer, in a hurry, is likely to convince himself quickly, being quite sure of what he wants to do, quite sure also that he can always sell and get out. It is still wise, even through all the rush, to know what is good Caribbean location, good Caribbean construction. A condo not oriented to the breeze, can become just as much air-conditioned living as a house built facing the setting sun. Some condos have been built by unprincipled speculators — also in a hurry. The deck may be plywood with a concrete wash, rather than steel reinforced concrete cantilevered. The whole thing may look comfortably American, while Americans are quickly acquiring a preference for Caribbean taste. Don't expect to furnish your condo with 'stuff from back home'. The rapid population growth in the Caribbean is resulting in discernment between old and new, dowdy and smart. If you are anticipating an unbuilt condo, the advice that applies to an unbuilt house and site applies also to you. Think — will your site which is only five minutes from the shopping area now, after five years be in the middle of the developing traffic jam? Many of the islands have roads carved out of rocky hillsides: they can not economically be widened. It will be well worth a rental car to spend a day driving 'downtown' on some of the already developed islands.

FIVE
Mindsweeping is
the start

If you take advantage of the climate and the simpler way of living, the cost of a house can be less than the equivalent space on the mainland: not the equal space but the equivalent in living functions. This is probably the most important reason why you should rent a while before building – to give yourself time to study the new way of life.

Much of the roofed floor space, for example, need not be fully-walled, just half-walled, or less than half, then screened.

Your enclosed rooms can be smaller, by mainland standards, but you are now privileged to disregard those mainland standards. All the outdoors, all year round, is living space.

You need less furniture. Furniture is lighter. Part of enjoying your newly earned life is learning to become freed from things.

Even wealthy West Indians have homes smaller than they would have if they were living on the continent. Unliveable cold weather outside requires larger living space inside.

Houses are less used as status symbols. Merely by moving to the Caribbean you have proved you have made it. The best status for continentals is that they no longer have to care about status. The fact is, if you build a house that is more than you need, people are less likely to think you rich than that you did not take time to think thoroughly through what you were doing.

Try to think West Indian. Recall that some of the cities in the Caribbean were old and wicked when the Pilgrims landed on Plymouth Rock while looking for Virginia. The West Indian manner has evolved out of centuries of experience. It has much to offer. Please don't get a friend 'to do a little sketch' for you, a bit of misplaced Florida. Resolve from the first quiver of enthusiasm to have a local architect, engineer or draftsman – or all three. You can hang any 'design' on the basic structure from the outside: Trinidad gingerbread, Florida box, country cottage – that's all wig and eyelashes. Get the torso right first. A house designed from the outside will have an inside to match. A house with the right inside can have anything outside from Japanese pagoda to King Richard castleate – and you can see both on St Thomas!

Do not start by thinking of a pretty picture in a housing magazine. First: think wind direction. This locates your large openings – facing the breeze. If you did not locate the breeze while on your site, you can do it, less accurately, on a land map. You need the breeze inside your house twenty-four hours a day, every day, not merely during daylight hours. Next: think rain directions. This decides your quick means of closing. Third: think sun – the western, blazing setting sun of late summer and autumn. This determines where you need the greatest roof overhang with the maximum shade; the hottest months are really not bad except for the few days of total calm. Even then, in the shade it is pleasant. Think overhang – all the way around. Make sure it's about four to eight feet wide – on the east to control rain, on the west to control sun.

Steeply pitched roofs are to make snow slide off, for example in Scandinavia and Switzerland. In the dry near east and the US southwest the indigenous style is a flat roof. The steeper the roof slant the less overhang you can have because the roof line keeps on going down. Flatten the roof and a longer projection is possible.

No matter where you build, your house will reflect your way of life, from an igloo to a Windsor Castle. Take time to get to *know* your new way of life. Take time to make sure you don't saddle your architect with 'home-town' notions and yourself with a house that will not foster your new island freedom. The most subtle and significant differences are not immediately apparent. Life lived mostly inside stresses large rooms and storage for seasonal furniture and clothes. These values differ from life spent mostly on decks and in play clothes. There is little need for a dining room with a long table where people prefer to eat outside on benches and at side tables, even for dinner.

Space- and view-starved city dwellers who insist on opening their house to the western view probably spend the first year erecting awnings and trellises to keep out the afternoon sun. Those who skimp on roof overhang go to the expense of Scotch-Tinting their windows. Inside, you are doing things mostly with your eyes down. Being cool is all important. The balcony where you sit to enjoy the view does not have to be on the open side of the house. It merely needs to be on the side with the view.

To make sure of these basics, it is sensible as a first step to take the architect or engineer to your plot. After you have located the breeze, the rain and the western sun, talk about the cistern. There are a lot of things that can be varied on a cistern. Unfortunately, they are not architecturally interesting.

In the islands, the first thing you build is a cistern, unless you choose a rain-blessed island with piped water or a proven sweet-water well. Even with a well, you may need a cistern for security storage. Normally a cistern provides all your water from rain. The initial cost seems high, but forever after you will have no water bill.

Also, while you have your architect and if possible your builder on the site, mention any rocks you want preserved from the bulldozer. Building some of the huge rocks of these volcanic islands right into your house produces exotic effects. Just keep in mind that a rock conducts water under it. This is why natives of the islands plant avocados and bananas downhill from rocks. If you do incorporate a natural rock into your rooms, be aware that it can cause severe leakage during a storm. Have it downhill or ditch it right from the start because many a man has spent his days after the first storm trenching around his favourite rock in the living room.

The purpose of the foregoing is to try to free you from concepts that have no value here. You do not start with a kitchen to please Her and a workroom to please Him. You start with a cistern for a year's supply of water.

Cistern size

The size of your cistern is not universally agreed upon. The figure for continentals is always greater than for islanders. No matter how a continental tries, he never can exist with as little water as an islander. For one reason, his guests will not let him. Many a host has contemplated murder upon catching a guest, while shaving, using an eight gallon flush to dispose of a cigarette butt.

The other consideration is rainfall. The figure given here is for areas such as the Virgins (US and BVI), for Anguilla, Statia, the ABCs and other dry (40 inch rainfall) islands. In the interior of Puerto Rico, Dominica and St Vincent, examples of wet islands, you could go for a smaller cistern with the expectation of more frequent rainfall. But I would certainly check and double check that rainfall figure on your property.

The size of the cistern has to be in ratio to the roof. The proportions can be calculated by an engineer. There are variables. In general, one should reckon on 20 000 gallons for a family of four continentals, for a year's supply. This assumes 40 inches of rain during the year. This allows for a quick shower and a sign over the toilet, 'On this island in the sun, we do not flush for number one'. A family of two with an occasional house guest will get along quite well. If you have a grey water system to augment this for toilet use, you'll be affluent!

Some areas of any island may not get 40 inches; others a little more. This is one of the variables. Learn your rainfall.

Assume a 1000 square foot of roof for a two-bedroom, two-bath unit. This encloses the essential covered area without an overhang. If you include the overhangs, you get about 1500 square feet. The size of the house, of course, determines the total. These figures are safe averages. If you design a small roof, that is, a multi-storey building, you may not be able to fill a 20 000 gallon cistern.

For example, a small narrow house may have no more than 800 square feet of roof. Such towers have been built by unseasoned young architects.

You also need to estimate how many visitors you will have and how many months their visits will total.

It is terribly difficult to write in detail about the whole Caribbean because in detail it differs so much. As a whole, it is fairly uniform – uniformly beautiful, uniformly temperate, uniformly non-censorious and accepting. But all that horrendousness about cisterns is just Chinese upside-down, where the rainfall is ample. Take St Vincent and St Kitts, for example, which are pretty much in the centre of the ample rain area. Even little villages have piped water from a reservoir. They build tanks (cisterns) above ground and separate from the house then pipe into the house.

But it's cisterns again in the Grenadines. There is no paradise – except on a three week holiday.

Staggered building economy

On nearly all islands you may be able to benefit from the generally permissive personality of the Caribbean. It is a widely accepted practice that young men go off-island, mail their wages back and get friends to build them a house as the money comes in. Partially constructed houses are common, especially on the emergent islands. It is not necessary to lock yourself into a total, completed structure if you have reason to spread out the construction time and the cost. The Caribbean is so overrun by rich foreigners that government officials, if treated with genuine respect, seem to empathise with someone not overly wealthy who wants to enjoy their world. At least, I have found this, as have others who are long-time residents. Your decision could be to build the minimum and enlarge it later against rising costs. An owner who is capable can do a great deal of work himself, incidentally, earning a surprised respect from the local people. He can start with one bedroom and add others at his own convenience. But the total design should be submitted for government approval at the start.

A roof is relatively inexpensive. You do not have to enclose all the area that is roofed. Snow won't blow in. Just screen it. Enclose it later, if you need to.

A cistern can be designed to have two parts. A second part can be built later. This is a costly method, but you have to decide whether you want the total expense at one time or spread out. A compartmented cistern has advantages. A wall down the centre is relatively inexpensive, but if you have a crack it permits repairs without emptying the whole cistern. Cleaning also can be done without the inconvenience of totally emptying it.

The two basic figures from which to calculate your variations are 20 000 galls for four continentals and 1500 square feet of roof. If you use a recycling system for toilet water, your cistern may be about one-third smaller. But you face possible breakdowns in the recycling system. A non-do-it-yourself owner may be wise to adhere to another maxim: as few mechanical devices as possible; opt for the larger cistern and skip the recycling. If you foresee the paving of a road or parking area which may fill a grey water cistern, engineer your plumbing with two valves connected, one with an unfinished spur line. You can then switch the toilets from grey to sweet, or vice versa, according to need. A toilet is the largest single user of water. Shop around for the kind that flushes with fewer gallons.

The cistern does not have to be under the roof, or the floor, although this is the design most frequently sold to foreigners. The narrower and taller the cistern, the less the evaporation – and the greater the objection from the builder. Actually, a cistern can be fifteen feet high, without changing the reinforcing specifications: a useful thing to know if building on a hillside with the cistern below your house. You may have to change builders to get it. A cistern can be used as a wall on the west, for example, to buffer the afternoon sun. Then the top can be additional catchment. Or the cistern can be used under the house with the top slab being part of the floor slab. If this design is used, be careful where the manhole is placed. When the manhole is in the living room floor, it can become a repeated annoyance: the handles trip people. Dirt collects around the edge because you cannot have a raised lip. Place the manhole in the pantry or off in a corner.

On a hillside a tall, narrow, long cistern can be downhill and form a support for the house to span from cistern to hillside. A downhill cistern can make a level building area on a steep hillside. Mainlanders sometimes shy away from a steep site because of their inexperience. But consider the many houses built on hillsides around the world. There is no problem. Hillside living has a zest all of its own.

The point is, a cistern should be thought of as more than a water storage tank. It can be a house support or a wall against the western sun, or a sun deck, or the base for a small second floor hobbies room or hideaway. Contractors more than architects tend to view cisterns unimaginatively as a part to be got over quickly – preferably stuck underground, where, incidentally, cracks and weeping will not be detected.

Hip roofs are popular throughout the Caribbean. They can be built cheaply. They are comparatively easy to build. The flat concrete roof, well established in Puerto Rico and Florida, is more efficient. It can be slanted toward one large downpipe. Gutters, the buggaboo of home-owners, can be moulded in concrete. Galvanised gutters rust. Plastic gutters leak.

The ferro-cement roof is recent, also successful, IF the builder understands it. The idea comes from the cement boats of World War Two. It consists of two layers of hardware cloth with cement squeezed down – thoroughly – through the first layer to a solid, smooth, bubbleless layer of cement on plywood. Then the hardware cloth has to be very thoroughly immersed in cement with a thin layer of cement over it. Next, the second layer of mesh is again immersed in cement and all is smoothed over. Gutters are made by turning up the edge of the roof all round. If the cement is not squeezed thoroughly into the hardware cloth, the roof will leak. The ferro-cement roof does not have to be flat. On Virgin Gorda there are many designs of peaked roof in ferro-cement, which are successful. There are also some that leak.

For the west wall, the consideration is a long roof overhang for shade. You can see some houses with glass doors facing west for the view. The owners eventually either extend the roof, or put up a trellis or awnings, which the wind and sun destroy. Alternatively they live with the curtains drawn and the doors closed to keep the curtains from flashing out like tongues and knocking over anything they can reach during gusts of wind.

If the top ten inches of the west wall immediately below the roof is left open but screened you have a clerestory. The air rushes through the large openings of the east wall, swirls up to the clerestory, and wooshes out west. An architect protested this would leave a glut of stale hot air at the base of the west wall. It was built despite him. The house is never without a breeze, never hot on the stillest, hottest days. The construction tends to create a breeze inside even if none is outside. The entire house is fan shaped from northeast to southeast with no two walls parallel. Each room has a slightly funnelled peri-meter. This creates a venturi type of airflow. The architect spurned it. The builder cried over the difficult angles at the west. The neighbours come to sit and chat on hot days.

In a West Indian house air is and should be a moving, living thing. You can design it. After all, the delicious air is one of your main rewards for moving to the Caribbean.

One house has doors opening northeast and southeast, the arc of the prevailing wind. By opening the door to the breeze and closing the other, air can be circulated around the whole house, because the bathroom, on the west, opens into the north bedroom and the south bedroom, and acts as a funnel.

The choice of window material is a never-ending argument. Glass louvres need cleaning. Wood and metal louvres keep out the light, plunging the room into darkness during rain showers. But, if the overhang is four to five feet, windows need not always be closed. Doors with wooden louvres need screens for they are in effect windows in a door.

The classic West Indian way to open a wall is by a series of solid wood doors arched at the top, usually for gracefulness. Inside the wood doors are full length screen doors. The wood doors open out against the wall, out of sight from inside. This provides a usable blank wall inside between the doors. The doors can be spaced more closely by making the wood doors bifold. They take only half the width when open. Such doors not only create the romantic indoor-outdoor atmosphere typical of the West Indies, they are most economical. The wood doors eliminate the need for storm shutters. They are often named hurricane doors. They permit a fast battening down of the house for security. They require no storage as do removable hurricane doors. For the genuine article, see the original doors on Golden Lemon Guest House on St Kitts. Main Street, St Thomas, has many good examples.

Too much glare is an easy mistake to make where light is plentiful. When someone says, 'There's too much light coming through that window', step outside where the light is even stronger; you will not find it too much. Glare is juxtaposition of light and shadow within the eye's range. When the iris of your eye is trying to open in order to see into the shade and trying to close in order to fit the light coming in, both at the same time, you get pain – from glare. The wall with a window should be light coloured. The wall opposite the windowed wall can be as dark as you want.

The wind is strongest from the north; so northern openings can be smaller. East is main ventilation: take all you can get. The south wind is weaker, except fitfully in showery weather. Windows can be large but should be adjustable. On the west have the heat-resistant wall with a clerestory as high as possible under the roof. The kitchen built against the west wall needs no stove hood. The clerestory whisks out the steam and heat.

Even so, on nearly any island you can see houses built with little regard to the air, with rusting gutters and open to the western sun – the owners were in too big a hurry to learn – and the architects were trained 'at home'.

Well, now we have a cistern with roof large enough to fill it: protection against the western sun by a heavy wall or roof overhang: ventilation by opening the house to the east with varying size openings on the north and south sides and on the west by a clerestory and well-shaded windows under maximum overhang.

Now is the time to enclose some areas.

To quote the senior BVI government draftsman, 'The worst mistake continentals make is overdoing the outdoor-indoor living. That is, they don't do it right. The open structure needs to be done with adequate care for insects and the climate. It needs adequate screening.'

In the several sectors of the Caribbean, the prevailing rains come from a slightly different direction. In most areas the rain comes from the north and east. From the west it is infrequent, but when it does come it is what boatmen call 'funny air', unpredictable. But the mountains shape the rains for each island. Some have williwaws, sudden gusts, especially off St Lucia and the Grenadines. Some islands are out of the hurricane path, such as Trinidad, whereas Puerto Rico has a strip called a hurricane path or tunnel or slide. This does not mean it necessarily has hurricanes, but it seems to react in a certain way during September and October. On the other hand, the Virgins depend on a few near misses, called 'cistern fillers'. You should enquire of old-timers from which direction the rains are expected at what time of year, and plan your maximum overhangs and shuttered doors accordingly.

On each island you will note that the knowledgeable people tend to close the house on two sides. Examine the inns and beach bars and see where most of the rain comes from. One architect on Tortola espouses a 'closed core', particularly suitable to the needs of a family who will not go into full retirement for a few years. The plan is to build the largest floor and roof you can afford and then cluster lockable rooms along the north and east. The remaining space under the roof can be visually enclosed by a very short wall and screening. When the family is off-island, the movable things can be put into the locked area. In the large screened area the furniture is built in or too large to move and weather-proofed.

The idea of enclosing along the east does not contradict the principle of opening the east to the breeze. The enclosable room along the east would have the large doors for ventilation.

Corridors, stairs, patios, atriums and showers need not be roofed. That's a lot of floorspace out from under when you add it all up. Virtually all Caribbean inns and hotels take advantage of the saving. Furthermore, it's romantic. Sometimes the roof overhang is used as corridor with a partial wall or lattice.

Stairs, for any but the largest buildings, are usually uncovered, and outside. Lounges and dining areas need only a low partial wall and screening. Throughout the islands you will find the most sophisticated inns and hotels making full use of the romantic – and economical – climate. This use of a partial wall, or no wall except tall plants and screening, was calculated by Harmon Associates of St Thomas to save up to 50% of wall cost. Unfortunately, their booklet *Virgin Islands Report* is now obsolete in its figures, although still valid in the principles. Wall only 50% of the roofed area. Put what you save into a larger roof and floor space. A copy of the book may still be available in the St Thomas library. You can experience the relaxing expansiveness of this design at Caneel Bay Hotel, St John; Treasure Isle Hotel, Tortola; Little Dix Bay Hotel – and all the inns and North Sound resorts, Virgin Gorda; The Beach Club, Palm; Young Island, St Vincent. Innumerable examples of broad open terraces you find anywhere, but these are not what the Harmon mathematical formula alludes to. Nor are the broad decks of private homes, unless they are consistently used as a conventional room. An unwalled room has a roof, in anticipation of rain, but also an immediate recognition of a limited function. It's the dining room. Or the games room. Or the hobbies room. It has furnishings intended not to become wet, which will be left in place during rain showers because of the roof design.

Bathrooms in the Caribbean permit truly imaginative treatment. Let your mind ramble. Your house can. In countries where pipes freeze, all the pipes are clustered near an inside wall. Where space is costly, all appliances are jammed together in a small room.

These conditions need not apply on a tropic isle. Forget them.

By separating the three functions of a bathroom, you can save the cost of a second room. Who washes at the basin and showers at the same time? If the functions are visually separated on a little larger floor space, with screening walls, two or three people can use the one room simultaneously. Removing the shower from the basin and the toilet is more popular than separating all three. Putting a shower of stone or other outdoor building material in the corner of the bedrooms seems to be gaining favour. If the guest bedroom is given a shower with access from the outside, with a foot bath, you save a lot of tracking, plus the expense of an outside shower.

Caribbean closets also invite imaginative treatment. So few people give them thought. Bedroom closets are sometimes freestanding in the function of room-dividers. They may be latticed wood or suspended shelves. Shelves can be strips with air flowing through. Shoes and foldable items lie, ventilated, on the shelves not in drawers. This retards mildew, discourages things that live in the dark, saves money and avoids sticking drawers. However, in a kitchen closet you may have one shelf tightly enclosed with a light bulb to keep salt, spices and condiments dry. Build it in from the start to save the nuisance and cost of 'where can I put the crisper?' later. Some of the lovely little guest houses on the three little Dutch islands have ventilated closets from years back. The cottages of the prestigious Bitter End Yacht Club of Virgin Gorda have only free-standing, open closets.

You do need one belligerently enclosed closet – the Owner's Closet. This closet should be built solidly into a wall with a tight fitting door and a high quality lock. The roof should be attached from the inside. You need a shelf enough above the floor to admit a typewriter or portable sewing machine or most valuable hand tools; a hanging bar for seasonal clothes; a top shelf for boxes of whatevers. If you plan to occupy the place for short visits and rent as frequently as you can for years, the Owner's Closet is for your non-rentables.

Every expatriate, renting or not, needs a place to store northern clothes while he is on island; island clothes while he is on the mainland. Be sure the Owner's Closet is:
a) large enough for things you don't want broken;
b) insect and vermin proof;
c) dry;
d) secure.

Of course if you have rented to a thief even a steel lined closet will not keep him out. Yet one more precaution is worthwhile: a box or drawer or compartment or disguised place, secure and fireproof. Banks on medium and small islands usually do not provide safe deposit boxes.

On dry islands, free standing bedrooms use space as acoustical insulation. All four walls can be of louvred panelling. The three functions of the bathroom, separated, are grouped under one roof.

The bedrooms are clustered around it. This design is good for the delayed construction of a family not expecting to retire for a while.

On wet islands, free standing rooms are – well, one owner keeps an umbrella at every door.

There are other ways of delayed construction. You can build the living-kitchen/bath units and use hammock and sofa beds on the rest of the floor. The house acts like a family 'cabin' until the required bedrooms are finished. This pattern permits families with many children to start earlier. On Virgin Gorda about half the houses in one settlement were built with two bedrooms and other rooms half above the cistern, the rest projected out to posts. Later the space in front of the cistern was enclosed as bedroom, bath and additional rooms at the whim of the owners. Jumping to the other extreme of the Caribbean, the builder on Palm says, 'Construction of the walls and roof with general purpose room so householders can get inside with minimum expense, then adding non-loadbearing walls to suit, is a sound way of getting a holiday home now at least expense.'

The above is not intended to denigrate low cost housing. It merely reflects admiration for a sentiment expressed about nine years ago by a native British Virgin Islander who has consistently built high quality, low cost guest facilities, Anderson Flax. 'The Caribbean should not be only for the rich.'

Solar heater

The solar water heater is such a complete success in the Caribbean, it should be as much a part of your initial plan as a front door. It does not have to be on the roof. (Screams of objection can also be taken for granted.) Some solar heaters are mounted on the south wall from which the water rises from the collectors to the storage tank by thermosyphoning. No pump is required. Prefabricated units varying in cost from about $800 US to $1000 US, plus installation, are available on several islands – Puerto Rico, St Thomas, Tortola and Florida. However, new sources come aboard overnight and many sail off the same way.

The following is not a recommendation, nor a reference, merely an encouraging fact. Some home-owners have built their own units.

One man, not an engineer, mounted the water supply tank from a recreation vehicle under his pitched roof. Then he used 36 inches of half-inch copper, enough 30 inch sections of straight tubing to equal

36 feet, a copper backing sheet 38 inches × 36 inches and a 6 inch deep wooden box covered with flexible, translucent fibreglass polyester and insulated with one inch thick pressed fibreglass backed with aluminium foil. He made it himself. In addition, there was a puttylike adhesive to stick the tubing to the backing without wrinkling the copper plate and a pile of fitting T-clamps, sealing compound and valves. The whole business was shipped out of the United States in a bicycle carton. The cost in 1981 was $207.42.

Windmill electricity

Windmills for driving generators are not the absolute success of solar heaters. Their mechanism is more complex; however, they are in use here and there. If you have your heart set on an undeveloped area the windmill is worth looking into.

Choose local materials

Local materials will give you a home that compliments its environment. Furthermore, the local material will probably weather better. Most of all, you are likely to end up with local materials as a matter of delivery. So you may as well try to like what you see.

Don't hesitate to ask home owners and builders. People on little islands are friendly. Materials vary suddenly, due to many business fluctuations. With on-the-spot discussions you may know better what is available than your architect.

The foregoing is the advice of architects, engineers and draftsmen. The next chapter contains advice from home-owners.

Building a residential/rental

This market looks good for a long time. It lies between the tyro-condo buyer and the retiree home builder. Many single people want to have a Caribbean life but are priced out by tourist rates. They are crying for new small, nice quarters. Also breakdown between two families buying one house is, predictably, high. One of them gets stuck with a too large house not designed well for renting, i.e. with separate cooking.

Whatever, design for excessive water use: you don't scold renters. Design a stunningly efficient studio room with everything. There's one on Virgin Gorda where the owner, a real estate woman, lives in winter while renting the large house above. You can rent to yourself part of the year or to a single or couple. In your later, married children years, this rental becomes a family overflow room.

SIX
Advice

Although the people responding here have completed different kinds and sizes of houses, their observations are remarkably uniform. Here are the voices of experience combined.

Don't be in a hurry. Speed is expensive. If circumstances are forcing you to leave where you are now – rent! Don't try to push your house construction.

When construction finally does start, one of you should make frequent appearances. Do not hang around and watch the men. That makes them nervous. You will seem distrustful. But show up when pipe outlets are being located. Check the location and size of doors. In the late stages of the interior you may be asking for some detail not familiar to the men. They may misinterpret a blueprint.

When you do get a contract with a builder, insist on a finishing date. If for no other reason, you can keep the contractor from taking on other jobs before he finishes yours. He might try to squeeze both jobs into the same time, thereby delaying yours. Nice guys turn into the most pathetic pigeons.

Choose a local architect or engineer. Too many mainlanders fall in love with the climate then bring plans from 'back home'. Ironically, the worst houses are those built by continental builders doing their own homes. Invariably the workmanship is superior. But the lack of adaptation to the Caribbean is hideous: large rooms with small windows; dark panelling, dark wooden floors, finest parquet, great for northern Canada; cute kitchens full of curlicues – marvellous for storing ants.

Eventually, the northerner's ideas have to be thrown away. Then the owner – to save money – is likely to make the second mistake: he depends on a contractor and tries to bypass architectural plans. Do not depend on a contractor for plans. They are not imaginative men. Invariably they will suggest what is easiest to build.

Get a barrister to check the actual width of right of way. 'For instance,' speaks the voice of experience, 'a right of way could be for a man and a mule. That provides not more than six feet.' Many islands still are in the stage of a hand-shake agreement that the boundary runs from a certain rock to three feet south of Mrs Vanterpool's back door. (Don't let disillusionment become discouragement.) This is the reverse of the coin. The obverse is life as it was 'in the good old days'. Most Caribbean islands have the qualities of the prairie towns of Canada and the US when people were scarce and morality was 'old fashioned'. Go slow. Stay pleasant. Be friendly. But – don't assume a Cadastral Survey includes all the requirements for finished use of land. One needs to be as cautious and thorough on an island as anywhere else.

Take time to be familiar with the site, the slope, the rocks and the run-off. John Randal McDonald, an internationally established architect with much Caribbean experience, emphasises the need for each building to 'belong' to its surroundings; to be compatible with its site as well as the needs of its users.

The home-owners still speaking

A   Learn the direction of the wind – all year.

B Learn the noises – by day and by night.

C Anticipate what the next neighbour will build – in your line of view, your wind.

D Learn whether mosquitoes or flies will be a problem during some months; these can influence basic design. (Remember the warning by the senior government draftsman, 'The continental's major mistake is inadequate screening.')

E Take time to develop *complete* specifications. 'Fine plans are the key,' says one owner. He proved his right to this opinion by completing his large house within the time and budget contracted for.

F 'Of course you should have the site chosen before any planning, any daydreaming, because the site gives insight into what kind of house you will have,' says another owner, still commenting on the subject of complete specifications.

G Be sure the architect incorporates into your plans the government construction specifications. They cover such details as using only fresh water to mix cement. Enough salt water can cause cement to crumble. It is a long-range bonus to get acquainted with as many government people as you can, as you have excuse for seeing. Your sincere questioning now will be flattering. Keep in mind many of these countries are very young, and they have only one level of government. You never know!

H 'Determine with the architect the plan and the cost – in extreme detail. (You've heard that before. They all say the same.) Let the architect specify locally available materials. If you don't, be prepared for delay and disappointment.'

I Minimise exterior painting. Be realistic about corrosion of metals. 'The wind and seaspray are your constant houseguests,' remarks one owner. 'The beloved prevailing wind will continue to prevail – over everything.' By accepting local materials you not only reduce problems, but end up with a house more in harmony with the environment.

J 'Specify rough finish,' another recent owner advises, 'because that is what you will get anyway. Fine sanding is not local tradition. Mill finish is more in keeping and if you get to a clash of opinion – just how fine is "fine"?'

K 'Everybody spends more than he intends.' This conclusion is universal.

Home-owners strongly urge you to contract for a fixed price.

They also advise you to include a penalty clause for the termination date. In order to do this realistically, insist on a firm starting date from which to calculate the termination – but – here reasonableness dictates that the owner take time to learn island ways. This is essential to sanity. Know the holidays. They are many and different from mainland holidays. For example, Puerto Rico celebrates the US holidays plus some Caribbean holidays. St Thomas, so much smaller, is dependent on Puerto Rico in many ways and there the people need to know whether Puerto Rico is in business on certain days. But the US Virgins have in addition to the mainland holidays their own island days. So, for business purposes on St Thomas you need to be aware of three sets of holidays. A damnable nuisance, until you yourself begin to celebrate all of them, and add a few from neighbouring British Virgins! Isn't that what you would like? One long holiday?

Learn the problems of shipping to an island: this may take an afternoon to learn and months to believe. Know the dependency of your island on the neighbouring island for trans-shipment. This is as serious as learning one-way streets in a big city.

You have two reasons for learning island ways: first, you will be more able to establish reasonable dates when you make agreements; second, you will not become so uptight. Much of your delivery is dictated by sea and wind – neither of which give a hoot how uptight you get.

More advice on a positive note: owners hold the universal conclusion that Caribbean people are wonderfully friendly, except for a few islands that have been spoiled . . . 'but don't push time'. If you are going to gather from an island its full beautiful, relaxing reward, you will have to learn an island's time sense. No island is ever going to learn yours. You may as well begin before you build.

a) Any date promised implies 'Wind and sea and God willing' – and all at the same time.

b) Any time given for delivery, or an appointment, means: not possibly before that hour or day.

L 'Make your contract with the architect, then don't make any subcontracts with the contractor.' Owners seem to be more vehement on this point than any other.

M 'Never believe that a change made by a contractor will not cost you anything.' The universal advice is to refer the slightest request for a change to the architect: this is why you hire a local man.

N 'Make sure all payments to the contractor are certified by the architect.' This same warning, put slightly differently by a different owner spelled out as: 'Wait until your house is completed before becoming friendly with anyone. You may be on the site more than the architect if you are renting on the island. Do not let this lead you into displacing the architect in his responsibility for approving changes. Better you should stay away altogether'.

I agree with everything – time, local materials, depend on architect – and I would add more.

O Have your lawyer check the title, the access *and* review the contract. If anything goes wrong – let him argue it out with the contractor. I was mighty glad of a lawyer when I did have trouble with the builder. Be sure the lawyer knows your contract.

P Get competitive bids: the difference can be ridiculous if one of the builders is new to the expatriate market. The bids on a road were $38 000, $52 000, $108 000. Ask for three bids because some of the available builders may not bid if they think the house is too complicated. The house bids were $191 000, $195 000, $208 000.

Q The architect should supervise but if he cannot or will not, you can apply to the American Institute of Architects for a form for supervision. There are also 'Quantity Survey, Project Management and Construction Companies' to supervise, if the architect does not.

'I am strong for local materials; as little paint as possible and as little wood as possible.'

R 'I would strongly recommend going with a builder from your island, even if an off-island builder sounds a lot better. The off-island builder ferried his men every day and never put in a full day's work – "the seas were rolly, the wind was high, one man was late and held up the whole boatload".'

Before you choose the local builder, you can watch him work. Who is really supervising his work?

Again, watch out for the lowest bidding builder. He may become the most expensive.

Ask your neighbours! 'Two of mine said "Don't use him" but I did not ask why. I used him. Now I know why!' The experience of those who have been through the builders may be more important than the bids. There are little things like putting in a bonus for early completion, then being reasonable about the penalty for failing on agreed completion. While you're being reasonable, pushing off the completion penalty date, you're assuring them the bonus. Some builders can't spell too well, but they sure can count. I agree with those who went before – 'If you're in a hurry, don't start!'

S Whatever portion of your house a contractor starts, don't pay him until he completes. Even to the last doorknob. Listen to this man cry. 'They didn't have the right operators for my windows. Such a little thing. I said, sure I'll get them. But if your contractor can't find a part – neither will you. I was six months before I got, from Miami, the right operators for the windows.'

The summary

This is the same from every home-owner.
'Don't hurry!'
'Stay cool!'
'Don't expect continental speed.'
'Quality is excellent, but islanders do things differently.'

The islanders are honest. They are friendly – provided you stay within the island way of doing things.

Do not keep asking when something will arrive because there is only one answer on an island, especially a small island. 'The boat fetches when she fetches.'

Regarding work schedules: wages are lower than in the US and Canada. Men stop to chat. Gardeners usually arrive early enough for a little bite under a tree, then stop again for elevenses. The emphasis is on humanity, not mechanisation. On any island you can hear about well-intentioned foreigners who arrive bubbling with the desire to 'uplift' local conditions. They start by over-paying, upsetting the local wage balance. When the wages in one group go up, they go up in all occupations. Then the merchants have to raise prices to cover their increased costs and soon you may be complaining about the rise in prices, forgetting that you caused it. It is far better to let the local people run their own affairs. They may prefer humanisation to mechanisation – tea at eleven rather than an efficient day's work. You can use your energy more profitably to control non-cooperative newcomers with loose purses.

It goes for condo buyers, too

If buying into an unbuilt condo, learn as one guide to quality, what cement is used. Puerto Rican or Venezuelan are o.k. Some Haitian cement, as an example, is said to crumble in ten years. See if the floors and deck are steel-reinforced concrete or plywood with a cement skin.

If the building is already tenanted, ask for a list of previous owners. That's no more than asking an applicant for references.

Think this is silly? In the USVI a whole wall collapsed in one condo occupied for years. Another opened a slit big enough for the breeze to blow through.

Watch out for the new builder who will be gone next year. There's a Caribbean species evolved from the boat business. Whether you plan to live in it yourself part of the year or to rent it wholly, you still need to have it built right!

Always keep in mind the first and last piece of advice of those who have built before you: 'If you're in a hurry, don't start.'

Come to the Caribbean – by all means come, but remember – don't bring the place you're leaving with you.

SEVEN
What to do while waiting

About-to-be retirees ask a lot of questions. This chapter contains some that are asked most frequently, and some that are not, but should be.

Periods of waiting intrude, no matter how well you plan. You have to wait for your land purchase licence; wait for the Government approval of house plans; wait for your contractor to begin – and to finish. Before all these, there is the interminable wait for R-Day.

The waiting we all wish for you is the best time of all, looking for your island, followed by the priceless time of opportunities while renting. These are the times to find answers.

Answers specifically on *Cost of Living* are in Chapter Ten. Although the first question is usually about the cost of living, the subject is delayed in this book because so many factors influence cost; factors which become modified by your attitude and knowledge of island people, island ways and places: a desire to become radiantly healthy can reduce your food budget for example. The nine chapters preceding are a prelude to judgements you may exercise in Chapter Ten.

Frequently-asked questions

Furniture

Islands without duty – you can bring in as much as you want. Dutiable islands do you a favour: they motivate you to throw things away. Most islands name a set value such as $2000 of furnishings per adult and some lesser amount, perhaps $500, for each family member under eighteen. The value is based on the *Used Rate*.

Consider this procedure: put your undecidables in storage for a year. At the end of the year, if you can't recall what is in a certain box, you have your answer. Storage usually provides for part to be shipped and part to remain longer.

Antiques

The artificial, monetary value of an antique is what someone will pay. Try to insure an antique in the Caribbean and you will find its value is the replacement cost of a new piece of the same use. Other expatriates, to whom you might want to sell, already have theirs or have cured themselves of the addiction. An American Hepplewhite desk, estimated to auction at $2500 in New York or Philadelphia, was insurable at $500. Even in San Juan no dealer would handle a piece so large because travellers could not take it back as luggage.

However, if you really like a piece and want to use it, that is reason enough for bringing it. Good antiques seem to hold up in the Caribbean climate as well as in the north. Just don't count on selling.

Antiques can induce culture shock. Our furnishings, with antiques, arrived on the St Thomas of 1967 in two huge crates, so large they were hoisted to the third floor and swung on to the deck where I dismantled them slowly. Soon we decided to move.

The 'Leading Mover' of those days arrived with a naked stake truck – and not a rag or scrap of paper for padding. The big items would not be bent around the stairs so they were hoisted down again like hay from a barn loft. That Hepplewhite desk! That centuries old teak table! That Pembroke maple dropleaf!

We were unprepared for the island's custom of stacking and

repainting scratches later. The table of ancient teak carving swung into space, wrapped in a blanket and a mink stole. The desk was heaved out in my cashmere overcoat. The Pembroke wore sheets. The rest of the bedding was stuffed around in the stake truck, bouncing from hill to hill.

A few years later it did not matter. The mink stole, never worn again, went to line a daughter's parka. The cashmere ended up neatly folded in a transparent bag and placed, like a Hindu corpse, on the pyre that was the public garbage bin, in the hope that an islander bound on a quick trip to the States might recognise an overcoat.

This digression about our stuff is not gratuitous: large pieces, especially upholstered, do not accommodate to the breezy, carefree life of the Caribbean as well as the indigenous bamboo or rattan which can be seen and priced on the 'hub' islands. I would like to ship my mink-cashmere level pieces back to the children, but freight rises in recent years have equalled off to the antique sales value.

One family, with significant experience in selling a house at inflated rate, then using the increment to build another which incorporates their experience, has in their third home everything which does not have to move, built in at the time of construction.

Entertainment equipment

Place-settings for twelve, huge Thanksgiving platters, items from those 'Let's have them all in and get it over at once' days, are used so seldom they can be borrowed.

Female retirees get smart fast here, especially when they quickly sense that 'Now next week it's your turn, Maddy', is not the manner among freed souls. Except for the rich, who do not do their own pre-paring, the people who settle in the Caribbean are prone to measure time spent in whomping up a big table party against three days of cruising in the sailboat. There's no comparison!

Local sources

During one of your earliest waiting periods you might check the shops on nearby islands. You could save yourself a lot of trouble and money. Many of the funny looking little shops, which at first glance resemble a warehouse hit by a cyclone, have stashed away amazing inventories – if you are looking for locally popular items. Coming from the west you certainly ought to give Puerto Rico, St Croix and St Thomas a good going over and always enquire the cost of freight. From the east try

Guadeloupe; if nothing else you will gain a realistic value of replacement for your shipping insurance.

Add to the replacement cost: crating, which has to be waterproof when going overseas; overland freight from your present home to the pier; warehouse charges if you do not time the trip precisely with boat departures; possible transhipment from the hub island to your island; land transport from the jetty to your site. The total rubbed on large and heavy pieces magically reduces their desirability.

The current craze for buying 'previously owned' and the increase in freight have changed the economics of bringing furniture. Do bring your favourite kitchen knives, and the best quality wind-up clocks because of the frequent electrical outages on growing islands.

In consideration of all this, take a new look at your children. Some of them have nested. But be prepared: some retirees have admitted to an itty bit of a shock upon learning the ungrateful brats don't want the old junk either.

Certainly bring the small things you handle – pictures, rugs, music, hobbies, tools, mementoes, things to kick under the guest bed. People hold on to these things. Buying new furniture gives you a shot in the arm. Many people enjoy the change.

Shipping furniture
Start at the end! I repeat, start at the island end. Don't first pick a hometown agent and hope he will target a jetty somewhere 'down there'. Be realistic. You are moving out of his area. He correctly anticipates that he will never see you again.

Track the handling from your island and work backwards. This way you can give the continental shipper precise last-minute off-loading information. They all say they know – but – do it yourself. What shipper in the north knows where the jetty is on Nevis or Tobago or Bequia? He probably won't really be clear whether the Caribbean is in the Bahamas or vice versa. One shipment from Ohio, under the aegis of one of the 'best movers in the world' who could ship anywhere in the world, did just that. His clerk assigned it to Puerto Rico because she 'could not find a reliable agent listed for St Thomas'.

Give the name, address, phone number and any regional identification of the best mover (according to those who *really* know) on your island, to the continental agent and get a contract for delivery (date) to that island agent. Don't accept a contract with the tailpiece, 'Local source to pick up', or some such buck-pass.

The car

Should you bring it or buy one on the island? The decision is controversial. Circumstances vary on each island; freight, shipping distance, cost of a new car, distance to hub island, duty, national quirks, etc.

The following ideas will give you a working base from which to depart.

To learn the real value of your present car to you on the island: deduct the cost of shipping (get this from a garage manager or real estate office). Deduct the import duty. (See the section on duties and customs, page 89.) Duty can go as high as 20% of used value.

While island hopping find out what resident expatriates paid for new cars – anywhere, but most probably on the hub island.

In fact, the monetary value may be your least consideration. Over the years, when you are on a fixed income, the cost of replacement and repairs will be increasingly important. The height of the wheel clearance on unpaved roads is important. The number of people who can be squeezed in besides the perpetual cargo is important. Miles per litre are less important. When the island is small the price of petrol is higher, but then one uses less. Typical prices are given in *Cost of Living* (Chapter Ten).

Service is all important – unless you can do it yourself. The local boys do. Somehow they get the job up on concrete blocks. If that does not appeal to you, learn which brand can be well serviced on the island. This may determine whether you bring or buy.

If you have to send to your hub island for a part, remember de part fetches when de boat fetches and de boat fetches when .... Or you have to get the part flown in. Or a friend may bring it when he returns from an off-island trip. Decide you're just crazy about the styling of the brand that keeps spare parts on the island.

It must be rustproof – new or used, rustproof.

If you go for a softtop, a sunshade or car port, in four years you can save three to five hundred dollars.

Car insurance

This differs from one group of islands to another. There's a national political twist as to which companies get the franchises. The British think you ought to favour British companies. The Americans think similarly only with different spelling and flag. It's all the same in the end, just don't count on bringing your old policy and transferring it.

What's the cost? It could be cheaper in the islands. Driving is usually a lot safer – there is less traffic and slower speeds.

Financial reference

Establish local credit as soon as you can. For one reason, you need to uncover any local pukker-snatches. For example, cheques of US bank branches in the British Virgins did not clear in the USA. A branch manager did explain this, more or less, but that did not help the cheques. The second reason is, just as mainland people prefer a cheque from a mainland bank rather than from the Caribbean, comic as it may seem, islanders feel safer with a cheque from somewhere they know. British, Canadian and US banks are all over the place. You might, however, feel more at ease with your bulk finances on an island you know well. In which case, open a checking account on St Thomas, St Croix or Antigua. Even so, a branch with safe deposit boxes on Montserrat or the Caymans could be convenient. But Mahnomen, Minnesota may sound as far out as Basingstoke, Hants, to someone in Kingston.

To bring your pet

Make an application to the Chief Veterinary Medical Officer, Agricultural Department, Government Officers, 'Capital City', 'Island'. You will need a vet's certificate of health as well as up-to-date rabies and distemper injections. The biggest variation among islands is determined by whether an island has facilities for quarantining. If the island lacks them, then you probably will be asked to quarantine your pet before leaving, and present proof on arrival. This is the reason for making your application at least six months in advance. Then add a couple of months for the postal service. Before deciding about your dog, you may want to learn about heartworm and tick fever. Dogs seem not to be bothered by the change in climate, even woolly beasts.

Duties and customs

Except on the ex-Dutch islands you will encounter customs. They may be collected at the airport, at the jetty or at the post office. If you wait until they are not battling with tourists, I think you will find them gratified that you have questions. Ask specific details because that's all they have, a book with percentages. You will find a page at the end of this chapter where you can make notes beside the items –

appliances, electric tools, tinned food, building materials, etc. Sometimes you can uncover interesting social emphases. In Tortola, for instance, hay for a cow is not taxed. The same hay for a riding horse is taxed. Some cuts of red meats may be taxed, whereas poultry is not. The reason is that cows go to the mass population and riding horses are for the few privileged. *Fillet mignon* is hotel fare – but chicken is the poor man's Sunday dinner.

Non-working luxury items will carry the highest tab, maybe 20%. Usually food is non-taxed unless it is tinned, then it is possibly 5%.

Governments

Getting to understand the local organisation can save you frazzled nerves and money. It is also interesting because the government of small islands is so unlike anything you have encountered. Furthermore, the friends you make before you develop a problem will be your friends in later need.

The islands are structured similarly with different names for the departments, except of course those which are long established republics or departments of France. One member of the elected Legislature of the British Virgins is Ralph T. O'Neal. He can not only laugh at himself, he can laugh at his environment. He describes his own BVI Government structure this way:

'There is a bit of interlocking and overlapping between the Government Departments. For example, in order to get a licence under the Non-Belonger Land Holding Regulation Act, the application is processed in the Ministry of Natural Resources and Public Health, but the actual licence is recorded in the Registrar's Office, not in the Land Registry. When the licence is completed and the land is transferred, the transfer is registered in the Land Registry.

'To get approval to construct a building the application is sent to the Building Authority and this, under the Ministry of Communications, Works and Industry, although housing, is under the Ministry of Natural Resources and Public Health. However, it may be necessary to get planning approval, and the Town and Country Planning is under the Chief Minister although Land and Surveys is under the Ministry of Natural Resources and Public Health.'

If you get lost along the way, just follow the white rabbit.

The purpose of this digression is to suggest that 1) at first you do need a solicitor for all paper work, fees and stamps, and 2) to illustrate for you the fact that a tiny nation of maybe 75 000 (Antigua) or even 17 000 (Caymans) or even 9000 (Bonaire), half of whom are children, carries an administrative burden greater in proportion to its size than a multi-million people country. There is a whole inner-structure and a whole outer-structure to staff. Furthermore, there is in effect only one level of government – no municipal government, no county government, no state or province government.

All retirees are warned: stay out of politics! This is wise advice for these young countries have many young officials. They are still organising their Boston Tea Parties and foreigners are not invited. But that does not mean you should not get acquainted. Just keep in mind while you are tiptoeing through the mushrooms that circumstances in mini-states call for patience and restraint. An exasperated complaint you write about the rotten garbage collection and a petition you want for a spur road off the highway may arrive on the desk of the same official at the same time. It's good to have friends in high places. In the small world, you try for a friend in the high place.

In order to get your various licences, permits and passes, you will need; three or four passport photos, so you may as well get them at the first opportunity; proof of financial sufficiency, which can be your bank; evidence of self-support without a job, which may be credit rating in your home town; a recent medical certificate, which may have to be obtained from a local source; a police record from your old home town.

Your waiting time can be creative, full of the zest of exploring, an overture to the songs of the future. As a guideline, here are a few questions that were asked at the New York VI Information Office.

'What kind of money is used in the BVI? Please send samples.'

'I don't have a passport, a birth certificate or a voter's registration card. Would my circumcision certificate prove my citizenship?'

'Can I bring a rifle? We'll be sailing and want to defend ourselves against sharks.'

'Where are the nude beaches?'

'What will the weather be like in the BVI in two weeks? Or do you think I should go next week?'

It is so easy to forget precise figures when you are excited that here is a chart to fill in for a permanent reference.

Cost of

Land tax..

House tax..

Death tax..

Capital gains..

Maid service..

Gardener..

Visa fee...

Income tax..

....

Import duties...

....

....

House insurance...

   Firm...

   Address..

   ....

   Telephone..

Services available
(note brands)

Car...

Fridge..

Freezer...

Microwave...

Stove...

(Bottled gas?)..

....

Water pump..

Blender, etc..

....

Washing machine...

....

Typewriter..

If service is not available on your island, note on which island it is.

Vehicle

Import duty...

Insurance...

Firm . . . .

. . . .

Freight . . . .

Cost of car licence . . . .

Cost of driver's licence . . . .

Where registered . . . .

. . . .

New car estimate . . . .

   Brand . . . .

   Freight . . . .

Rental car . . . .

Shipping agent . . . .

. . . .

Telephone . . . .

Real estate agent No.1 . . . .

. . . .

Telephone . . . .

Real estate agent No.2 . . . .

. . . .

Telephone . . . .

Preferred site: Plot No. . . . . . .size: . . . . . .Cost . . . . . .

Second site: Plot No. . . . . . .size: . . . . . .Cost . . . . . .

Furnishings shops

Item . . . .

Shop . . . .

Item . . . .

Shop . . . .

Item . . . .

Shop . . . .

Item . . . .

Shop . . . .

Item . . . .

Shop . . . .

Medical

Dr: . . . .

. . . .

. . . .

Emergency: ....

....

Main hospital: ....

....

Important Contacts
Barrister (attorney) No.1 ....

....

Address ....
Telephone ....
Barrister (attorney) No.2 ....

....

Address ....
Telephone ....
Chief Information Officer ....

....

Chief Librarian ....

....

Government officers
   Title .... Name ....

   ....

   Title .... Name ....

   ....

   Title .... Name ....

   ....

A most pleasant way to get the answers for your blank spaces is to look over all the expatriate homes and call on those that appeal to you. People are friendly where they are not jammed together. Any expatriate will be pleased to talk about his architect, his friends in the government and recommend suppliers. If you ask exactly the same question of each, you will be launched on research in the professional manner. Go shopping with a potential neighbour. This is the time to find out whether the island offers the bridge game, the dance group, the tennis, boating, painting or what-is-it you will want.

This is creative waiting – pretty soon you'll be thinking of 'my friends on the island'.

EIGHT
Accents, dialects and patois

Language in the Caribbean is not a barrier. English will get you anywhere, even where French or Spanish are the basic languages. Haiti, for example, where laughter and gestures form half the talk, or even in Guadeloupe, the ultimate, simple English will get you through, even down a long nose. As for the many accents and dialects, they are not so divisive as in Europe or even in Great Britain. They are just spice added to speech, as the nutmegs of Grenada and bay leaves of St John are to the total cuisine.

Certainly, not all West Indians speak a dialect any more than all New Yorkers speak Brooklynese or Londoners cockney. Most West Indian speech has a local flavour, the soft, musical quality generally admired in Latin tongues by Teutonic ears. Some writers (tone deaf perhaps) have referred to a singsong quality. This may reflect proximity to Spanish and French. For instance, the question, 'Where it is?', with a rising inflection at the end, is the same as '¿ Donde està?' If you hire local help you will get used to the lilting telephone question, 'Who it is?'

Some West Indian words predate current usage in North American, unchanged since the time of indentured servant and pirate.

If a transient visitor is misunderstood or misunderstands, the consequence is little. For you, a potentially permanent resident, what the neighbours really say is important.

These few words you will hear many times: the meaning is not quite as you might think.

Gap: is an opening into a yard, a road or a field. 'Turn right at the third gap' may be a direction given to you. It does not mean the third street. A gap can be a side road, a hole in a fence, or just a broken place in a hedge.

Mash: on the mainland is generally reserved for vegetables. In the islands it retains the full range of nuances of the original meaning: hit, pound, push or step on. During a car inspection, the policeman may tell you to mash the brake. Someone may warn you the sea mash up the beach. In which case you would go to a beach on the opposite shore.

Next: is used for 'another' and for 'second'. Your gardener may ask, 'You have a next shovel?'; the waitress, 'A next beer/soda?'; the storekeeper, 'A next pack of nails?'

'I have a sister in Ontario, a next in Manchester.'

Copper: is a copper coin. 'Give me a next copper,' means you need to pay one more cent.

Title: This is a particularly necessary word for a householder. Title means surname. Name means given name. 'What is your name?' 'Agnes.' 'And your title?' 'Braithwait.' If you say to someone, 'Do you know my name?' you may get a surprising, 'Oh yes – Johnny.' It doesn't take long to learn 'title'. Among experienced off-islanders you will find they know the expatriate's term. Avoid asking someone from an unsophisticated island for his 'last name'. It sounds suspicious, like asking an alias.

Make: is used to tell age. 'How many years do you make?' 'I make ten.' This is from Spanish.

Script: means a written message. It is important to avoid confusion. 'I will leave a script for you,' is used rather than 'note'.

Wash my skin: In many ways West Indian idiom is more precise than Euro-North American speech. To wash one's skin is more precise than to wash oneself. What is a self?

Reach: (boat language) means arrive, even for people. If you should offer a 'drop' and he waves you on with 'Ireachawready', sing out 'O-kay' and go on. He may call after you. 'Thank you, you're welcome.'

Some common words in the expatriates' countries are not used in the Caribbean. 'Swat' is one. Ask for a fly swatter at the local shop and you may get a blank stare.

A small incident some people feel deeply. They enter a shop and are greeted with unsmiling seriousness. They have not learned this is respect to strangers. Then if their request is received with a bland stare – of uncomprehending – some people interpret the reception as hostile.

One word caused a homemaker, who was insensitive to language, to have a bad experience. The housewife told her Barbadian maid she wanted some soft, fluffy dried plant like pampas grass.

The maid suggested she use 'arrows'.

The lady dismissed the suggestion – 'Much too stiff – like sticks.'

A few days later the housewife triumphantly showed her maid exactly what she had wanted – an armful of the feathery tops from sugar cane.

The maid said nothing about the 'arrows' – the word for sugar cane plumes. But the maid felt 'disrespected'. True to pattern, the lady never knew how she had offended. But after the next payday she was minus one maid.

Goin' for a sea bath? a local may say as you pass in a bathing suit. There are very few openers between an islander and an expatriate. The levels of contact are seldom equal and informal. 'Sea bath' is a pleasant conversation starter, stranger to stranger or near stranger. It can hit the unaccustomed ear as 'Gon fo seebaa'.

Many women and elderly islanders cannot swim. They do not think of swimming as a pleasure. They go to bathe. This is not true of the younger set. Listen for *seebaa*. It means going for a swim.

Give me a drop? You may be accosted while driving, especially by someone who knows you and knows where you are going. A 'drop' is a lift, a ride. It is the same as 'Will you drop me at . . . . . .'. You could unwittingly snub someone who was beginning to accept you as a friendly neighbour.

Drop me by the coming gap: at the next opening.

Two flims to wash: this is here because it is funny. Many islanders say 'flim' for film. It's easier. Developing is a sort of 'wash'.

Generator plugged out: Anything that can be plugged in, can be plugged out.

This sampling reveals that some words are different and sometimes structures are different, for example plugged in and plugged out, instead of unplugging. Not all West Indian words that differ are so tame.

Some can be bombshells in a social situation.

Molest and **Pester**: have reversed emphasis. Molest is mild. You will see signs, 'Please do not molest the plants'. It would be proper for you to ask a teacher to let you observe her class, 'If I do not molest the children.'

But an expatriate man should just drop 'pester' from his vocabulary: it means to keep after a girl until she gives in. I was asking a shop clerk a lot of questions until she became irritated. I said, 'I just want information. I didn't come here to pester you.' I left in a hurry!

Woman: has a temporary tone, bottom of the ladder. Better to concentrate on 'lady' – which can mean wife, mistress or girlfriend.

Amusement: often has this context: 'He wife vexed at he girlfriends. She want all he amusement.' 'Entertainment' comes closer to TV watching.

Front: requires forethought. A man's front is – his front! You can bring a conversation to a startling halt by such an innocent comment as, 'He had better keep up a good front'. Neither the Puritans nor Queen Victoria made it in the Caribbean, so the pause would not be caused by your introduction of that masculine matter but more likely by the abrupt irrelevance to what you were all talking about.

Grammar in all living languages is continuously changing. West Indian grammar goes back to Queen Elizabeth and King James. Although it has been modernised, some of it is as it was four hundred years ago. While the English buccaneers were bringing their language into the Caribbean, scholars were trying to firm up its syntax. They were deciding whether the declension of 'to go' should be 'he goes' or 'he go'. The mainland took the form 'he goes', whereas some parts of Merrie Olde England retain, and the islands opted for, 'he go; they goes; he don't; they does'.

The verb *to ask* had two roots in early English: ascian and acsian. In the Caribbean, you will sometimes hear *acs* preferred to ask, as in 'I acsed him'. It sounds a bit bloody if you don't know the background.

In the use of pronouns, the islands and the mainland have gone in opposite directions. The mainland trend is to say him, her, us instead of he, she, we; 'It's him; it must be him' and 'Us girls had better stick together'. 'That's them'.

In the Caribbean the change is the same type of grammatical revision but favouring the subjective case rather than the objective: 'I give it to she.' 'He told we.' 'She' and 'he' are substituted for *hers* and *his*. Spoken fast it gets a little thick: 'She takes she baby to he.'

West Indians working with expatriates quickly accommodate to mainland grammar. They have always lived in a multi-lingual ambience.

Dialect similar to West Indian is heard in the offshore islands of the Carolinas. They were settled by tobacco farmers from Barbados, in the seventeenth century.

Anguillan Charlie Gumbs once answered me in the same biblical tone. 'Old? Why that tree was old when I came into knowledge.'

Another elderly gentleman from that stratum in Barbados who have preserved British heritage, when asked how his exclusive compatriots got along with the run-of-the-mill Bajians, was the one who replied, 'We does business with them but we does not roost with them.'

Also in Barbados I knew one of God's finer creations, Mr Oliver Grimes. Handsome and impressive, he had a complexion and voice that could have undone the Virgin Queen. Mr Grimes was a man of substance who drove a cab, like other landed down-islanders, to get US dollars. After he handed my wife into his taxi, she fluttered a moment then whispered, 'I'm not dressed for this occasion. I need my train and tiara.'

Mr Grimes stopped his car in the middle of a narrow street to speak with someone on the sidewalk. Horns blew. Traffic piled up. Mr Grimes descended from his seat, moved back to the first horn-blower and pronounced, 'Can you not see that I am conversating with a lady?'

Instantly our taxi seemed like the lead car in a funeral procession.

Mr Grimes taught us much about Barbadian life. Some children scrambled in front of the car, followed by yammering adults. Grimes mashed the brakes and muttered, 'Redlegs!' Immediately he apologised. Curiosity inflamed, I wormed out of him that the first slaves on Barbados were Welsh prisoners of war shipped by Oliver Cromwell – as slaves, not as indentured servants (the first Africans arrived a quarter of a century later). Working in the sun of the fields they acquired the name 'Redlegs'. Their descendants still rate it. Apparently the Welsh did not roost advantageously.

The Dutch for many years were the chief carriers in the Caribbean. They created a Creole English as a universal language so that plantation managers could talk to Africans, as well as the Welsh, Irish and Scottish recipients of Puritan righteousness. This may explain the prevalence of 'de' for 'the'. The same phenomenon is heard in other areas settled by the Dutch: the New York 'de', 'dem', 'does' and 'toity-toid' of Flatbush. The Dutch simplified the English, which may explain the uniformity of verb forms in a language hideous with irregularities. Pronunciation was also simplified. All As are broad – 'pahsengers', 'bahgs', 'fahst', 'mahn', 'pahntry', 'pahssport'. These accent variations are not as difficult as some in the US and Britain. However, when it comes to patois – shall we say it is not as difficult as Chinese?

Patois is a decomposed French spoken on former French possessions. The English conquerors bothered to educate only a top layer. The islands flipped back and forth between the two kings so frequently they probably thought it was not worth making a deep change. Lower economic levels were permitted to continue with French in any way they could understand. In general tenses were dropped except the present. Time words were added for future and past. In practice it works just as well. The verb has only form regardless of person or number.

Here's a petite sample phonetically:

ô nom ho = a tall man

ô fam ho = a tall woman

If you listen carefully, the patois sounds like a Frenchman talking with a mouthful of very hot potato.

Where English has always been spoken, the jargon is not patois but more of a slang, an argot, intelligible although not understandable by a stranger.

In Barbadian, for example, the words sound like straight English that have acquired local meanings.

Floats are small flour cakes made with lots of baking powder.

France is a small expletive: 'What the France you think you doing!'

Freeness is something given, especially food or drink as: 'At the end of the meeting there will be a freeness.'

Coming is an important expression of time throughout all the Caribbean. 'I'll see you Friday coming?'

If you say, 'I'll see you next Friday?' you are being less definite – some Friday, another Friday. A day worker could mistake this to mean he will be called when he is wanted again. Ruth Sherwood could add it to her Hundred and One Ways to Lose a Man. The difference between 'coming' and 'next' is worth learning.

Trini-bagian-ese is less intelligible than Barbadian. It is more of an argot, breezy, slangy, secretive. The difference is that of proper Barbados and flip-polyglot Trinidad.

Fatigue: 'Doan gie me fatiguem man, or ah buss you mout.' = Don't ridicule me. Don't tire me.

Beat back: 'Nobody can beat she back when it come to lying.' = Nobody can out-lie her.

Benzine: rum

Twin brother: good friend

Use yuh kidney: use your head

There's a whole dictionary of Virgin Islands' words. Thousands of people live happily in the Virgins without knowing the book exists. You would never need to know all these jargons and dialects, only to know that they exist so that when overhearing you won't think senility has set in 'an yo spigidim over strumoo bout head swatsy'.

Some of the speech differences are pure delight, especially the tendency toward the picturesque. Asked his opinion on premarital sex, a man answered, 'Only de knife know what is in de pumpkin.'

NINE
The way it's done
. . . local customs

Visitors seem unanimously to value West Indian manners. The tranquillity, the gentle speech, the quiet ways all result from island custom. The current influx of strangers, especially tourists who have no time to learn island ways, is causing concern about how long island customs will endure the conflict from outside.

Even bigger Caribbean countries are worrying a little about preserving people-to-people harmony. Small affronts eventually brew the broth for international irritation. Mexico, for example, a robust country with strong traditions, produced a book entitled *In Mexico It's the Custom, Senor!* Many passages apply equally to every island of the Caribbean.

One fits exactly – 'Handshakes Are Handled with Care'. (Reprinted from the booklet.)

'North Americans who like their handshakes hearty are frequently surprised at the delicacy of the Mexican brand. It's not because a Mexican couldn't give forth with the bone crusher grip if he wanted to. It's just that according to the Mexican social code, the light handshake is in better form.'

Writing from the eastern end of the Caribbean, with a slight inferiority feeling among the world's giants, it is consoling to have Big Brother Mexico also concerned enough to say, 'In Mexico It's the Custom'. In the West Indies, too, it's the custom.

Sadly, the visitors' own efforts to be pleasing cause more serious misunderstanding than any other facet of behaviour: the perpetual smile. This 'social' smile is more true of Americans than of Canadians, least true of the British, whose tradition leans towards reserve. Among the West Indians the polite face to show to strangers is one of sober attention. The smile is reserved for something funny or someone well known and liked. Interestingly, this is not so on French Haiti, less so where Spanish culture is basic, mostly so in the British Commonwealth islands and most intensely where tourism is recent. Of course, store clerks quickly learn to interpret the visitors' behaviour, as they learn many accents. Unfortunately, the visitors, untutored by cruise guides, or travel agents, or anybody, often conclude the 'natives are hostile. They don't like me'. Any individual clerk or taxi driver may be suffering a headache or adjusting to an unwanted pregnancy; they may have any of dozens of reasons for not smiling, one of which it is true may be umbrage at the 'plastic smile'. The real damage comes not from the overly straight face nor the overly effusive face, but from the interpretation: 'the natives are not friendly. They don't smile. They don't like me. They don't like white people.'

It is such a pity to start out carrying the curse of past generations. Islanders have always come in such an assortment of colours that they are less obsessive about skin colour than they are about behaviour. From the beginning the French and Spanish policy was to encourage inter-marriage and produce Creole populations. The English and the Dutch held to a policy of separateness. The basic reaction to skin is different in the Caribbean. Certainly there is a learned skin prejudice. Visitors who bring it with them teach it. However, for the expatriate who looks to a Caribbean life, it is well to practise a little restraint upon first acquaintance. The smile will come, gorgeous smiles that seem to rise from the toes, all genuine.

Probably the second breach of custom one notices is with the words

'Thank you'. This is rapidly changing due to increased tourism from the US and the influence of the TV. However, on some of the islands, the more rural population do not say 'Thank you'. There are other expressions. And the Americans' 'You're welcome' apparently is quite confusing when 'Thank you' already is too much. The result can be amusing: ten years ago I congratulated a garage owner when he brought his equipment into a room from his former site under a tree. He stood in the middle of the floor and stared at me. He was a fierce looking guy, all beard and fuzzy-headed. I thought I had somehow insulted him, he seemed so to be struggling inside. Finally, he blurted out, 'Thank you. You're welcome', covering both options.

This occurred also when the *Maverick*, which I had been cruising on (more than ten years ago), rescued two Barbadian fishermen who had been drifting for six days with only the fish they caught and the rain in a tarpaulin. Our skipper heaved a plastic bag of food and a bottle of water to them. The two men, instead of pouncing on the provender, stood beside in heavy argument. Finally the shorter won and pushed the taller to the rail. He stood there so long, his chest heavy with what he had to say, that some of the passengers surmised he was going to make a bite for money. Finally he yelled, 'Thank you. You're welcome', giving us the maximum treatment.

The point? Even though English is the lingua franca of the Caribbean there is a lot of lingo in the lingua which should be accounted for before deciding the natives don't like you.

There's another custom that irritates exceedingly in the breach. There is no substitute for saying 'Good morning' or 'Good afternoon' or 'Good evening'. Even when you open a telephone conversation, not saying it immediately sets you up as a stranger.

This custom is also dying out – being murdered – especially among the TVised young. But you can't go wrong by adhering to it, boring though you may find it (as I do).

On my first visit to Antigua, years ago with a co-worker, we were walking on a narrow, dark street through a village – close together and down the middle, I admit. We were aware of dark figures on the doorsteps on each side. Just as we, cautiously, passed a few of these forms, a clear voice rose behind us, caustic with innuendo: 'Goooood ev-ening geeent-til-men!'

The simpler housing and quality of clothing in the Caribbean should not imply a lack of social discipline.

Even if this is not going to be your future homeland, the Caribbean is undeniably growing in importance to the western world. Failure to observe a little custom can cause significant resentment. There is a sort of reverse racism that goes to work. The local people think: they disregard our customs because they think they're better than we are, just because they're rich and white.

In this way, visitors can create for themselves the impression that the locals are hostile, when they are merely offended by breach of etiquette.

A retiree and his wife left their boat while he approached a group of young islanders on the corner. In his best back-home manner he said, 'Pardon me, please can you tell me what is playing at the movie?'

The youths stared at the ground in sullen silence. Finally, one muttered: 'Can't you say "Good Evening"?'

The visitor thanked them. Neither he nor his wife had heard that title so they walked to the cinema, giving the surly hoods a wide berth. At the marquee they found quite a different title. Only then did the man realise he had not been answered but had been rebuked for his lack of good manners.

Different manners are important in different countries.

Even entering a doctor's office, or any place where people are waiting, a softly spoken 'Good morning' will produce recognition all round. It's part of the friendly feeling people say they like in the Caribbean. The breezy little 'Hi' does not substitute here any more than an Austrian's 'Morgen' would substitute for a 'Hi' where 'Hi' is the custom. People would wish, can't he just once in a while say 'Hi'!

It is related that on one of the more populous islands, almost two decades ago, they were experiencing the onslaught of tourists. The police became so uptight about visitors who barged up and without a murmur of 'Good Morning', said, 'Hey bud, where's the ....?' that they froze, turned their heads and ignored the visitor. The situation became so tense the Chief called the police together and told them to think of tourists not as people but as walking dollar bills. Today, the island is generally referred to as 'spoiled'.

Another small convention comes at the end of a conversation, no matter how short. It is customary to say 'Okay' as you walk away. Outsiders, having brought the conversation to a reasonable close, turn and leave. This gives the impression of anger or rudeness. Try to remember a lilting 'Okay', even if you merely toss it back over your shoulder. You'll be rewarded by the pleasing chorus of 'Okays'.

It is ironic that the Caribbean should have been pioneered by pirates, ruffians and opportunists of most ruthless behaviour, yet the West Indians who remain, after the scions of violence have been outgrown, are a gentle people. They do not touch others, except when they are among intimates. The back slapping, the shoulder patting, is not returned by the West Indian and, under their patient exterior, it is not enjoyed.

The non-violent nature is still apparent, though being educated out in some regions. A typical West Indian incident occurred in a long line of waiting people. One of the men carried on his shoulder a twelve foot beam. As he turned, the far end clobbered the head of another man. The clobbered one pressed his head between his hands and said, in a soft voice, 'You mashed my head, man!'

The one with the beam accepted the accusation in silence for a minute then said, also in a soft voice, 'Was accident.'

Incident finished.

Fist fighting is something I have never witnessed in nearly twenty years, although I hear there occasionally are some on out islands. Four little boys were fighting under my window about fourteen years ago. Their fighting was typical. They stood face to face, heads thrust forward and yelled at each other while windmilling their arms up and down at the side. Their caterwauling finally got me down so I put my best calypso record on the record player. The kids looked around, listened and smiled, then in file danced on down the hill. Typical – dance first, fight later. Flailing the air while talking loudly is what one might call a common fist fight in the islands. When outsiders yell at each other and slap and push, being playful among themselves, they are sometimes misunderstood by islanders who have not been thoroughly indoctrinated. They destroy the quiet that is such a prized attribute of the Caribbean.

This is not in contradiction to the killing violence that has and does erupt. Crimes of passion are here what they are anywhere. The occasional organised, political violence is the uncontrolled outpouring of feelings by people who are inexperienced in expressing strong frustrations.

In fact, being non-judgmental is another characteristic of the area. An experience at a funeral tells the story well. I went to considerable trouble to squeeze into my one dark suit and finally was able to borrow a black tie. At the funeral was a man in dark trousers but wearing a sports jacket and a brightly coloured tie. Perhaps feeling vindictive about my own efforts to find a tie, I whispered to an islander companion as we left: 'Do the local people resent it when someone comes to a funeral dressed like that?' I was expecting a slightly scornful, 'He don't know no better'. She whispered back, 'Oh no. He doin' the best he can.'

There is comfort in an atmosphere where you know people will say of you, 'He doin' the best he can'. Non-censoriousness is a priceless area trait!

Approaching someone's home, in a land where all windows and doors are open all the time, except in rain, is practised with tact. If the place has a fence, it is proper to advance only as far as the gate then call 'Inside', three times with long pauses. If you receive no answer, the person is not at home or does not wish to be disturbed.

Even natives are now building with double glass doors. This places the obligation on the caller of approaching close enough to be seen from the inside but not so close as to see inside. It is extremely annoying to have someone, nose to the glass door, peering all around the room asking, 'Hello, anyone home?'

Even a policeman answering a call will pause at the steps and call, 'Inside'.

Where doorbells are not used, the call 'Inside' is the doorbell.

Now, just to take care of the defensive reader, some non-islanders do go straight up to the door, even the door of a native's house and tap. And they say, 'Well I did it. She didn't seem to mind.'

A deep-seated part of West Indian manners is not to show disapproval. This is a charming trait. It keeps the ambience delightful. It is sometimes a most frustrating trait. Your maid doesn't show up – and never shows up – and you won't ever know why.

While shopping you can encounter behaviour patterns that need understanding. You are not so likely to find them in a grocery store where expatriates shop frequently, as at a library or agricultural station or police station. One trait is: do not interrupt.

This contributes to the quiet tranquillity of the island. One shopper went up to a store-person who appeared to be the manager and poured out a stream of complaint. The clerk listened till the bitter end, without a sign of impatience. When the speaker finally burned out, the clerk said quietly, 'The manager is off-island today. He back tomorrow.'

Well-bred islanders do not interrupt. Even not-so-well-bred do not either. Listen to a group of mainlanders talking over each other. You will hear the difference.

If you consider this trait, combined with the manner of not smiling, while listening and, possibly with a little trouble over accents, you can see how the stranger might have cause to think, 'They don't like me.'

Another trait of the Caribbean is extreme literalness in speech. Take this instance: a man entered a long shop with many counters. The first counter was laden with ladies' underthings. He asked the salesgirl if she sold men's belts.

The giggling girl said, 'No.'

Remembering how precise Caribbean speech can be, the man asked again with improved literalness, 'Where in this town can I buy a belt for man?'

The clerk pointed to the last counter at the back of the store.

Generally in the Caribbean the people do not entertain inside their homes. This varies in proportion to the size of the island, to its cosmopolitan quality. But on most of the islands that one thinks of as 'really West Indian' the homes are smaller than expatriates' because they do not need to be so big – for one reason, they do not entertain inside. This is an important thing to remember when you hear someone beginning to become disillusioned. 'They never invite me to their homes.'

One custom West Indians have that established a sense of community quickly is not being picked up by many expatriates, especially those in developments. The 'House Blessing' is the local form of Open House. Usually the owner asks a minister – or lacking a church affiliation – a well-known friend – to read something appropriate about 'blessing this house and keeping it holy'. The service is as brief as you choose to have it, followed by juice and perhaps baked stuff. Not liquors. The announcement is usually by word of mouth and just the term 'A Blessing' on such and such a Sunday afternoon will be enough. It's a well established custom throughout the islands. Any responsible native will be gratified to give advice: the shopkeeper, garage operator, school teacher. He will also advise on which tree or lamp-post you should put your announcement. The occasion is inexpensive, very simple, sort of boring to a mainlander, but worth bushels of gold in public relations. Everyone has a chance to see your new way of furnishing and shake hands. No favouritism is indicated among guests.

Virtually all expatriates hold 'Open House' cocktail parties. A few invite locals. The occasion has no resemblance to the simple, non-alcoholic 'Blessing'. The West Indian 'cocktail' party stresses food, more like a mainland buffet. Liquor is cheap. No one is impressed. Food is expensive.

If a continental holds a 'Blessing' at his home he can then hold an 'Open House' cocktail party (which is by invitation) without getting the reputation of exclusive.

Several islands now have so many expatriate homes clustered together, cocktail partying each other – by invitation – that the term 'White Enclave', or 'White Ghetto' is appended.

In your studying, look as objectively as you can at the people in the 'White Enclaves' and those living 'out'. The attitude towards local customs is different. The people who think the local customs are quaint, or silly, or who are unaware that there are strong local beliefs, seem to be people most likely to begin feeling, 'They don't like me. They never smile. They never invite me into their homes. I don't think they're so friendly.' These are the people most apt to pack up and sell out in three years, leaving only a wake of bad feeling. It is too bad for them but it is even worse for those who are left to clean up the mess of their trail.

Perhaps the essence of the difference between Caribbean manners and mainland manners is that the Caribbean in many ways is still 'in the good old days, conservative, disciplined'. Isn't that part of the atmosphere you would like to retire into? It is vulnerable.

Ten years ago I tried to get some of the young men to call me by my given name. I got tired of being MR Hunt, as though I were still in the office. They wouldn't. Finally one explained: 'My grandfather would box my ears if I were rude to you.' Eventually they settled on the local term of respect toward the older person. I became Mr Syd. You'll always be on safe ground if you address shop personnel and others of brief acquaintance as *Miss* Agnes, *Mr* Rupert.

Writing about manner is writing about people's behaviour. There's no end. From one aspect, it is the most important topic in the book. It is your way of making yourself happy or unhappy with the people around you. These few pages are just a nod to the subject, because when push comes to shove, a sensitive person, wherever he or she comes from, will be sensitive in the new home. Unfortunately, the reverse is also true.

When you have earned the compliment 'You are polite', you have an achievement. Anyone rated by the local people as 'polite' has passed the test in the public eyes for being more than just well spoken. The island word covers a multitude of virtues – quiet of manner and speech; not over-tipping or showing off; not referring to advantages 'back home'; not touching or patting or poking the person spoken to. Above all, polite means not subtly giving off an aura of superiority. This time the meaning is not 'White Superiority'. It is the superiority of 'Bigness'. It is difficult for someone to avoid when all his life he has been backed by the rightness of some three hundred million fellow rich-educated-experienced continentals. (Anybody is rich who can spend a thousand just to get here.) The aura of self-assuredness can come across as brashness to someone who knows himself economically disadvantaged but feels himself to be, nevertheless, a gracious host for his own land.

One other compliment is a notch higher, coming only with time and probably when you least expect it: 'Don't feel that way. You one of us, man!' That is polite *summa cum laude*.

Perhaps this is a futile chapter. Those who need to be told this, won't listen. You who have the interest to read it, don't need it. In time you would sort it out by yourself.

Well, let's say this little sample is, perhaps, to help you find what you're looking for a little sooner; to hasten the time when you become one of us, man, in your happy retirement.

TEN
Cost of living full time, short time

The question about the Caribbean most frequently asked is, 'What's the cost of living?'

The answer has been postponed until this chapter because the best answer is, 'The cost is whatever you choose to make it.' This sounds irritating, rather like a brush-off. To understand, one needs to know the variety of sources available to even remote islands and the diversity of Caribbean living conditions. Some people live on boats, some have lavish spreads. Some formerly top-level impeccable ex-executives revel in becoming almost beach bums. One wife of an ex-law department head laments that the only time she can wash his one pair of play shorts is when he's asleep.

Hardly any newcomer can appreciate the variable factors enough to form a usable judgement. The most obviously sensitive to discretionary spending is the grocery bill. For true overall budget comparison, however, you need to factor in certain expenses which are changed by retirement: the cost of urban boredom; cost of holding a job; cost of keeping up with fashion; keeping up with competitive neighbours, fellow workers, friends; cost of recreation; cost of custom-dictated entertainment; the design and construction of your house – how maintenance-free, how easy to clean. These need to be estimated separately from the following common-place factors like:

1) transportation   2) taxes   3) clothes   4) supermarkets
5) entertainment   6) housing   7) insurances   8) heating
9) medical   10) medicines.

The grocery bill (edibles and non-edibles) in the US dollar areas is generally declared to be 50% higher than the States or Canada. Some say it is 100% higher. Both are true. It depends not only upon what you buy but where you buy. This is true anywhere. Why should it be different in the Caribbean?

In the Eastern Caribbean Currency area it can be halved.

Even on undeveloped islands you can have the fanciest meats that are catered to hotels, shipped from the same suppliers, ordered by telephone and delivered to your dock. Anywhere, it's nice to be rich.

Hub islands (Puerto Rico, Antigua, Sint Maarten, St Thomas, Trinidad and Curaçao) can be cheaper because of lower freight and handling charges on imports. On second level, emerging islands the price is higher by the cost of the additional transhipment from the hub and because of smaller inventories. However, you still have to watch for this: US goods sent into a British zone can be more expensive than equivalent British goods because the original British cost is in pounds. Third stage islands are likely to have the highest costs of all because of having the smallest inventories, greater shelf-spoilage and possibly carrying an additional 6% cartage from their big sister island.

An actual grocery record for one person in the British Virgins (a small island), in 1975, 1976 and 1977, averaged out at $173 a month. The purpose of this year-long record was to alleviate the unknown in the possibility of drastic loss of purchasing power, for any reason. Incidentally this did happen in the early 1980s.

The goal was to eat the most nutritious diet as cheaply and happily as possible. The menu included no liquor, tobacco, junk food, red meat and only a minimum of processed foods. It did, however, include fancy cheeses, top quality chicken, turkey and fish with an occasional rum for cooking and a wine for entertaining. In 1988 a similar record showed $300 to $350 a month — for one. This could be reduced by shopping monthly on nearby hub islands. No duty is charged on food.

In areas where a major craftsman earns $6 to $10 a day US, as in some of the ECC islands, the general cost of living, especially food, has to be commensurate with local earning power. In the US dollar area a craftsman may get $50 to $60 a day. Jamaica has a price freeze on labour and staples. Recent visitors ate well for $9 a day US, including liquor.

Barbados manufactures many excellent products priced by the Bajian dollar: softgoods, vitamins, essences. For example, 200 ml of pure vanilla essence from Barbados sells on Tortola (in a British-owned shop) for $1.45 US. An American brand vanilla extract on Virgin Gorda (in an American-owned chain-store), sells 118 ml for $5.45 US.

Following is a list of recurrent predictables with empty space to fill in the equivalent on islands you investigate. Figures given are average within the US dollar area.

Recurrent predictables

		'Your' island
Driver's licence	$10	....
Car licence (4 year old)	$50	....
P.O. Box	$25	....
Bank box	$30 to $50	....
Land tax ½ acre (USVI much higher)	$20	....
House tax (portion of rental value higher on developed islands)	$200	....
House insurance $60 000: 80% all contingencies. Going up fast. Best insurance is hurricane, fire-proof construction.	$727	....

Non predictables

Your national income tax   . . . .
Your island income tax   . . . .
Work Permit   . . . .
Bond for alien employees   . . . .
Sales tax land purchase   . . . .
Medical insurance (US)   . . . .
Income tax consultant   . . . .
Solicitor (land and house)   . . . .
Maid (high rate) $20/d   . . . .
Gardener (high) $30/d   . . . .

	Guess	Actual
House repairs	. . . .	. . . .
Landscaping	. . . .	. . . .
Uninsured medical	. . . .	. . . .
Long distance telephone	. . . .	. . . .
Clothing after 5 to 10 years	. . . .	. . . .
Ferry between hub and your island	. . . .	. . . .

(People tend to forget the cost of the last leg, eg fare from Toronto . . . . to Antigua. But then from Antigua to Union . . . . to Palm . . . .

House guests	. . . .	. . . .
True miscellaneous	. . . . . :	. . . .
Grocery (multiply monthly average by number in family)	. . . .	. . . .
Electricity	. . . .	. . . .

(Average monthly $65 to $75 US. One family's runs at $110 to $150. She has all the gadgets. He has extensive power tools, and is always maintaining his boat, enlarging his house. Higher electric bill should be deducted from savings in maintenance.)

| Petrol | . . . . | . . . . |

Retirement savings estimate

You really owe it to your future to anticipate these savings resulting from retirement life simplification:

1 Cost of boredom How often have you redone a room because you were tired of the colour? How many times have you bought clothes, not because the old were worn out but because you were bored with them? When I cut out, to my surprise I uncovered eleven usable suits and five coats with accessories, probably because I hate clothes!

2 **Cost of entertainment**   Island fun can cost nothing, or just fees for golf or tennis, or rental of movie cassettes.

3 **Keeping-up-with**   Nobody to keep up with. You got it made by being able to live in the Caribbean.

4 **Cost of holding a job**   Transportation (two, three cars?), lunches (downtown club?), donations (get your name in paper?), clothes (quantity – annual fashion?), entertaining (even with expense account there is maintenance of home facilities).

5 **Cost of cold weather**   Heating house, water; summerising house, car; winterising car, house – permanent, annual; two or three complete wardrobes.

6 **Vacations and holidays**   Daily living has holiday flare. Big bashes, such as Christmas, will be your own doing. Most islands make little fuss of anything but Carnival. Rather go fishin'.

7 **Cost of deteriorating health**   Not merely doctors, but drugs, pain killers. The slogan here – move to the Caribbean, live ten years longer. Air is your main source of nutrients. Water you can live without for several days; food a couple of months; air – four minutes. As you begin to feel better you gain the will to eat less, exercise more, reduce your addictions.

8 **Dry cleaning**   I can't remember seeing an establishment outside the US Virgins and Puerto Rico.

9 **Home-grown produce**   Significant gardening does not require expensive equipment as in the north. Also, local growers do not spray. Birds tell you when the fruit is ripe.

For retirees whose finances are marginal, going native can show high intelligence.

Initial cost is house and transport

Transport may be a boat or vehicle or both. Once you have shelter and transport, existence in the Caribbean is flexible and undemanding.

Now we come again to the irritating observation: the initial cost, also, is what you make it. The house, depending upon which island you choose, varies for the average two-bedroom expatriate type from

$50 000 to $75 000, low cost island; from $150 000 to $250 000, US, expensive island.

The averages given for the various islands are the best informed estimates. Since different government departments did the estimating, there could be, and likely is, variation in judgement. Remember costs go up each year; the Caribbean is a boom area; Caribbean prices do not drop for depressions. They go on 'hold' then rise again.

Anguilla has no average size parcel. A two-bedroom expatriate house costs around US $65 000. **Antigua** estimates expatriate holdings from 7500 to 10 000 square feet; cost: US $1.25 to $2.50 a square foot. Average houses cost from $120 000 to $145 000. Land is 'tight'. There is no beachfront. **Aruba** land is mostly government controlled with prices according to location. Construction costs run at US $150 to $220 per square yard. A 'modest but comfortable home could be constructed for about US $22 000' – government quotation. In **Barbados** an average home, including land, is US $100 000. Land and houses are available. In **Dominica** land costs EC $2.00 per square foot; construction costs are EC $80 per square foot. In the **Dominican Republic** a house costs US $50 000 up. In Jamaica a $\frac{3}{4}$ acre plot with a three-bedroom, three-bath house plus pool costs an average of US $180 000 (Tryall at Hanover). Prices are rising because expatriates are returning. **St Kitts'** usual size plot of land is 8000 to 25 000 per square foot and costs US $1.30 to 1.50 a square foot. House costs are US $45 to $60 a square foot. **Montserrat** parcels from $\frac{1}{4}$ to $1\frac{1}{2}$ acres are US $15 000 an acre; an average home costs $75 000. In **Palm Island** a $\frac{1}{4}$ acre plot with 80 foot waterfront costs $35 000 to $40 000, including the use of island facilities, club house, etc. A house sells for $65 000, with completed kitchen and bath, contracted. On **Saba** 300 square metres cost about US $10 000, a house about US $55 000. On **Statia** prices average out at $\frac{3}{4}$ acre for US $8000 to $22 000. Construction costs are $40 per square foot. A two-bed, two-bath house costs $48 000 to $50 000 US. **British Virgins'** prices vary from $\frac{1}{4}$ acre in a development for $20 000 to waterfront acreage for $1 000 000. An average size house costs $150 000 up. **USVI** prices range from $8000 for a bargain $\frac{1}{4}$ acre to whatever the market will bear.

The following is a sampling of costs most frequently requested by potential buyers. Not all islands are able to provide the same type of statistics. When an island reports in ECC, the figures have not been translated to US dollars because the fluctuations in the dollar affect the

ECC rates to such extent that the impression could be false. You can get ECC equivalents from a bank. Costs given are for 1983.

Electricity cost

Anguilla: flat US 18¢ per kWh. Antigua: 1 – 100 units ECC 40¢; 101 – 401 35¢ and so on down. St Kitts: ECC 52¢. Statia: US $60 average per month with all appliances. British Virgins: US 24¢ first 60 units, then 22.5¢. USVI: 9¢ for first 200 kWh then 7.4¢.

'Your island' . . . .

Petrol cost

Antigua: ECC $5 a gallon. Barbados: US $2.10 a gallon. Dominica: ECC $6 a gallon. Dominican Republic: US $2.57 a gallon. Jamaica: US $1.89 a gallon. St Kitts: ECC $4.70 an Imperial gallon. St Lucia: ECC $5 a gallon. Montserrat: ECC $4.7 an Imperial gallon. Saba: US $1.41 a gallon. BVI, Tortola: US $1.68, Virgin Gorda, $1.97 a gallon. USVI: $1.55 a gallon. 'Your island' . . . .

Hourly wage

1 Skilled carpenter or mason: Anguilla: US $3.50. Dominican Republic: US $10 per day. Dominica: low even within the EEC region. Jamaica: carpenter US $5 per day, electrician $7 per day. St Kitts: ECC $6. British VI: lower than USVI but much higher than ECC area. The BVI has over-employment which makes for labour bargaining. This sometimes costs up to US $10 an hour. Furthermore, some contractors add a high overload. USVI has personal contracting. You can find labour costs up to a half lower than on the mainland. However, the USVI has a labour union. It's all a little bit West Indiany.

2 Maids: The price of maid service is changing more than any other cost, so any figures will soon be out-of-date. Ask around in 'your island'.

Land tenure

This varies. You need to ask early in your exploration. It can be tricky when you buy direct from a native family. Anguilla is from individuals. Antigua is freehold. Montserrat is freehold. Palm sublease from Caldwell's 99 year lease. Saba is from the owner. The British Virgins several years ago underwent a cadastral survey to clear up confusion where ownership could be spread over fifteen members of a family some of whom were in foreign, remote countries. Boundaries were defined like 'from a certain rock to the back door of Aunt Eudoria's house'. BVI holdings are all right now but you should personally check details of boundaries, right of way and multiple ownership anywhere. USVI is like the US usually, no problem if you go through a realtor unless you face eviction rights. Then it's *caveat emptor*! On every island you need a local solicitor or attorney.

'Your island' . . . .

Land availability

Some islands tend toward government control, for example Aruba, Jamaica, The Caymans and parts of the British Virgins. Among the smaller eastern states, Antigua is the only one which declared a shortage of land. Montserrat, Palm and the other Grenadines have beach frontage.

St Vincent with its many Grenadines is cordial to settlers; however, there seems no rashness in selling land. The government seems to have a clear-headed desire to keep the island from being spoiled by rapacious opportunists, as does Dominica. Aruba, speaking for the ABCs, specifically states that their control system permits no speculation. The British Virgins have a strong fear of speculation and require a certain amount of construction within the first two years. It has clamped a 25% fine on would-be sellers who provided no improvement by the time of resale. More islands are opening to settlers. Anegada, a virtually unknown British Virgin, is undergoing a process whereby many acres of Queen's land (government land) are to be made available for sale.

All the islands require alien land holders' licences except Frigate Bay, St Kitts. They weed out undesirables such as racists, drug addicts and their associates and criminals, by the well-established West Indian practice of 'Your papers got lost – again'.

Income tax

In the US Virgins, Americans who transfer their legal address to the islands pay only Federal Income tax. This is paid to the island government. The money stays in the USVI. There are advantages.

The predominating income tax rule for most islands is that foreigners do not pay unless they earn in the island. Learn as soon as you begin investigating whether the island income tax is deductible from your national tax: some countries have a no-double-taxation agreement. The Dutch islands have a no-work-permit policy. A few have a graduated income tax on world wide income. There are slight variations on each island: Jamaica, for example, has a graduated income tax on only what is earned in Jamaica. Aruba (ABCs) taxes a resident of more than 183 days in a calendar year by a graduated system similar to the US but with much lower rates. For example, on $5000: single 6%, married 5.7%. If this can be subtracted from your national tax, it's a plus. Aruba has property and usage tax. Anguilla, Antigua and Saba have no income tax; Barbados and Montserrat, tax is the same for expatriates as locals. You need a book to detail them all. Which brings us back to the retiree's gospel – rent, rent, rent first.

Rentals

All the islands have rental properties, the more developed the island, the more the condominiums. On St Kitts a furnished house goes for $350 to $500 a month. On Palm a private house rents for $400 per week per bedroom. On Jamaica, new houses, super de luxe with maid, cook, laundress – are $2000 a week. But almost all islands have more 'romantic' accommodation. Jamaica, especially in the Negril area, provides privately-owned houses inexpensively. Little guest houses on Statia and Saba are loaded with atmosphere and intimacy with local neighbours. Anguilla has rental houses right on a beach. Hotels on Dominica are so inexpensive that you can roost with service for less than a furnished room in the northern islands.

It is ironic, but the Caribbean way of life that is best for you can reduce your cost of living. You need only a few loose, cotton clothes, a figleaf for swimming and, much of the day, a pullover or *guayabera* with slacks for 'dress', long sleeves and shoes for 'formal'. To get up with the sun is better for your eyes; it also saves electricity. Eating raw field-ripened fruits and vegetables is science's 'newly discovered' way of preventing illness – and it cuts the cost of cooking.

Breathing pure air; the best of all exercises, swimming; absorbing beauty, beauty everywhere – these are the highest recommendations for health. Free!

One more factor influences the lower cost of Caribbean living. It is impossible to detail but it is real and big. This is the financial burden of subcultures: drug addiction and its remedial doctoring, burglary, fencing stolen goods, organised crime's skimmed-off profits, political and corporate bribery, military over-purchase, overflowing jails, legally packed insurances, the frustrations of a society divided into hostile strata. All get paid somehow out of taxes. The stress is paid for out of deteriorating health, rising medical costs. Billions not taxed are added to the billions taxed against those who tolerate and imitate.

Island gross national products are too small to support much dishonesty. There are no sewer, water or school taxes. Only token armies and coastguards exist. There are no drug rehabilitation centres; no subsidies for ploughing under. The cost of one level administration is low. The cost of labour and produce is low. There is no labour grafting, no sweetheart contracts, no subsidising of pricing.

The economics of life are simple.

Of course there are drugs in the Caribbean. It has a major traffic lane – Columbia to Sint Maarten or the ABCs, to the Virgins or Puerto Rico, thence by 'diveboats' to Florida with scuba-tanks full of liquid cocaine instead of air on the return trips.

Small island budgets do not carry the burden of parasite subcultures because salesmen cannot sell where there are no customers. It's the 'fast lane' big spenders who provide the untaxed billions.

Theirs is the environment of anxiety.

Sun, sand, surf and above all simplicity produce the most delicious yawns.

ELEVEN
In the kitchen ...
recipes

What will your Caribbean kitchen be like? It is as difficult to define as Caribbean food.

From the earliest days, the dishes of the Caribbean have been a medley of favourites brought by the settlers from France and Spain, from England, Holland, Portugal and Denmark. Then this international smorgasbord was enriched by the fruits and roots of Africa. Later it was spiced with the curries of India, the dainties of China, and recently the exotic mysteries brought by the refugees from ex-Dutch Indonesia.

Gradually necessity, from the rapid growth of a labouring population, adapted these imports to the indigenous supplies, mainly cassava and tania from the Arawaks. Ironically, the Caribes are the only people who have made no permanent contribution to the Caribbean kitchen. They had a serious supply problem, their staple having limited replenishment.

The probability is that Yorkshire Pudding and bouillabaisse have been around the islands longer than bullfoot soup.

This international character, this overwhelming variety, will not encapsule the unique quality of your kitchen. There will be something more penetrating to your daily existence: the sweetness of the air breezing through an all-open kitchen; the all-but-forgotten freshness of mountain stream water, or the pure softness of rain water; sunshine flooding your counters with nourishment from the god of health himself. You will have no need for a tight, windowless cubicle, designed to keep winter out. You may even have a door to the outside – like grandma's. Under an almond tree you can sit in the shade to peel and chop and chatter.

This is today's true Caribbean kitchen, still in the nostalgic years of tranquillity, combined with the most modern fridge, freezer and microwave. Sun-ripened tomatoes all year round and in every month a tree-ripened fruit.

You will not find this kitchen among the expatriates as often as among the locals. It takes a little time to know such a kitchen is feasible. You can easily find in new homes the kitchens tucked back in a windowless corner, even fashionably tiled in solid black, or hooded over a stove venting toward the east. But this is for those in a hurry, too much of a hurry to learn that the Caribbean is a world of its own.

If there was ever an environment designed to make the kitchen a temple to health, here it is. Of course, the Caribbean has no law that says you can't eat yourself into an early death. On the other hand, the retiree's life of reduced tension and better food is expected to add ten years.

The next question that usually pops up is: How do you shop? And where – without climbing a tree?

Well, even on a medium small island such as St John or Saba or Virgin Gorda, you can put on your heels and drive to a supermarket in ten minutes, or less.

You will usually find your choice of famous brand canned goods from New York to Hong Kong, plus butter from Holland, Denmark, Ireland or USA. There will often be cheeses from Greece, Italy, Denmark, US, Britain or Holland. Sometimes, however, the selection is less: caviar, for example, is seldom more than Russian or Swedish, but a little deprivation enhances plenitude, doesn't it?

Islands with many smart hotels such as St Maarten, St Thomas, St Croix, Puerto Rico and St Lucia must have an unfailing top-grade supply of tourist fodder. Most of the wholesale warehouses maintain a little back door for local retail trade – prime ribs, this or that *en brochette*, such home-made, hand-made gourmet viands as stuffed and breaded crab claws, by the case.

Even in the adolescent Grenadines you can phone an order to St Vincent and the mail boat brings it twice a week. Truly, you need lack for nothing unless it's money. Then you have the local mom-and-pop stores with local provisions, priced for the craftsmen who make $35 a day. Once a month you can go island hopping, load up a cab and pile the deck of the local ferry with cartons. There is a great deal more than you would expect, and never find, if you were a tourist. Would you ever expect to find Texas quality barbecue ribs in Rosseau, Dominica? Take it from a Texas lady now returned to the BVI. 'It's good there! The open market is lovely and has all kinds of things.'

Fort-de-France has a huge outdoor market under a wrought iron roof that looks like a Victorian postcard. It has so much of everything it's fun just to walk through. If you have ever hopped on to a suburban train into a big city to shop, you can hop on to a local ferry and treat yourself to an afternoon in France.

There is one thing all these markets have in common besides varied and fascinating inventories; higher prices than you are accustomed to, probably. Not necessarily, but probably. However, this does not apparently bother the many retirees I have questioned.

'It isn't all that much higher,' says one retiree from the place where people say all that much, 'besides you make it up on clothes and liquor and lots of other ways. And it's such fun.'

That about summarises your International Shopping.

So much for the dull news.

Now for the good stuff.

A Californian on Virgin Gorda says, 'I used to import from Tortola on the same boat that served the Bitter End Yacht Club. The steaks were excellent, until I discovered I could get excellent steaks right here. Actually, the hamburger is ground here, no fat; better than in the States. The island keeps changing, you know, and new sources open up.'

Besides the supermarkets, the open markets and the wholesale convenience foods, you will have three sources of local produce: mom-

and-pop stores, neighbours who grow too much and your own garden. (Don't discount the neighbours. Garden produce here is not like on the continent. It keeps coming and coming and coming.)

Part of the fun of the small shops is companionship. They still tear damaged leaves off cabbages before weighing them. You can learn the news that really counts, such as whose baby was born with red hair. Get the inside dope on that sometime.

The neighbours can inundate you from time to time with bananas, papayas, soursops, pumpkins and potatoes as well as the fruits of successful experiments with seeds from 'back there' – radishes, turnips, carrots, oakleaf, tomatoes, parsley, eggplant – they all spring abundantly as though they think they are late and it is already mid-summer. What can happen in your kitchen is not covered in the cook-books. Just about the time when you have eight huge papayas stowed under the sink until you can cope with them, a neighbour's beaming face appears. 'Look what I have for you! Did you ever see such gorgeous papayas in all your life? Eight. I know you'll just love them.'

This is how one retiree, a nurse anaesthetist, a Lt. Colonel in the US Air Force, coped with papaya inundation. She decided to adapt the Arab *kousa mahshi*, zucchini stuffed with rice flecked with chipped lamb, raisins and pignola nuts, with spiced tomato sauce over it. Substitute papaya for zucchini, sunflower seeds for the nuts. But which Caribbean – East Indian, Creole, North African, Spanish?

She chose two large papayas to serve four each. She cut them length-wise into halves, without peeling them. Scooping out the seeds she saved them (life in the army had been hard sometimes). Papaya seeds can be pickled or used as capers. Since the papayas were semi-ripe, green on the outside, streaked with orange, yet still quite firm, they needed no pre-cooking. If they had been green and hard, she would have blanched the halves in a large kettle of rapidly boiling salted water until the flesh was somewhat tender. Then she drained them thoroughly. She put the halves cut-side up in a shallow baking dish and spooned in two varieties of filling:

Filling No. 1 (an East West Indian version)
1 tablespoon vegetable or olive oil
$\frac{1}{2}$ cup chopped onion
$\frac{1}{4}$ cup finely diced celery
$\frac{1}{4}$ cup shredded carrot
1 to 2 teaspoons curry powder

2 tablespoons tomato paste
½ cup water
1 cup cooked chicken, cut up
1 cup cooked rice
¼ cup raisins
⅛ cup chopped blanched almonds
Sauté onion, celery and carrot in oil until soft.
Add curry and stir into vegetables.
Add tomato paste and water: simmer 10 minutes.
Add chicken, rice, raisins and almonds, mix well.
Stuff papaya halves, bake in 325° oven for 30–40 minutes.
Serve with side dishes, for example: chutney, coconut, salted peanuts,
raisins, minced green onions, chopped tomatoes, crisp fried bacon.

Filling No 2 (West Indianised Arab version)
1 onion, chopped
1 lb hamburger (an Arabian would use lamb)
2 cups cooked rice
½ cup raisins
¼ cup soft sunflower seeds (inflation's answer to the pignola nut)
2 eggs, lightly beaten
Sauté hamburger or finely chopped lamb in skillet until hamburger is
browned.
Divide the mixture, placing one half in a saucepan to reserve for sauce.
To the hamburger mixture in skillet add rice, raisins, sunflower seeds
and stir to mix well.
Simmer 5–10 minutes.
Add lightly beaten eggs and mix thoroughly.
Stuff papaya halves and bake in 325° oven for 30–40 minutes.
Serve with sauce.

Sauce
Reserved hamburger mixture
⅓ cup tomato paste
1½ cups water
¼ – ½ teaspoon each of cinnamon, ginger, cloves, nutmeg
To hamburger mixture in saucepan add tomato paste, water and
seasonings.
Simmer while papaya is baking.

Now, that lady vowed she never cared much for cooking, there was no challenge; but she thought the papaya challenge was fun. A new world – that's what retirement should be.

A retired orthodontist never thought of cooking back in New Jersey, but here is what he did with an over-abundant crop of papayas.

Marty H. is especially interested in papayas because they provide more vitamin C than oranges and therefore are good for the gums. Every part of the tree also contains papain, a natural digestive, and tenderiser. Once the fruit is ripe, it in fact begins to digest itself. It soon becomes mushy and unpalatable. This was Marty's problem; he needed some ways of saving his crop.

He peeled a fruit that was just turning yellow, a lemon shade. For a 15 inch electric fryingpan, he used two papayas ten inches long (about two pounds). Here are the rest of the characters in his *dramatis personae* for:

The Toothsome Papaya
Half a stick of butter
2 tablespoons brown sugar
1 teaspoon salt
A touch of black pepper
1 large onion, minced
1 large sweet green pepper diced fine
2 cups water
Dice the papaya to twice size of sugar cubes.
Sauté in melted butter.
Add the rest of the goodies, cover and steam for 30 minutes.
Serve as a vegetable to about four guests, having anticipated that they will all want seconds.

And you still have a dozen papayas under your sink – football size, basketball size, softball size; yellow, green and yellow, all green. What will your Caribbean kitchen be like? A periodic papaya festival.

Now suppose lunchtime is rushing at you, here's a delicious offering – a potato salad made from green papaya with no potato.

Green Papaya Salad
Peel and dice (sugar cube size) a large papaya.
Steam until tender but not mushy. And watch it, Papayas have little

126

resistance. They hold out against you for a few minutes then – schlup.
You then make green papaya soup!
For each cup of diced papaya stir in:
Juice of half West Indian lime
1 teaspoon of olive oil
Let these three get well acquainted for an hour, then chill.
For each cup of diced papaya add:
1 hardboiled egg, chopped
$\frac{1}{4}$ or $\frac{1}{5}$ or $\frac{1}{8}$ onion chopped
(depending upon whom you will be kissing)
1 small stalk celery, chopped fine
$\frac{1}{4}$ cucumber diced
3 chopped olives
Salt, paprika
Optional: something spicy if you prefer,
a dash of cayenne, or a drop of Worcester-
shire sauce, or $\frac{1}{2}$ teaspoon horseradish. First
try the papaya without the spices, as papaya
flavour is extremely delicate.
After another hour, add mayonnaise or salad dressing – enough to
make the salad moist but not sticky.

Now let us suppose you have on hand some potatoes, which you may
as well learn to call 'Irishes'. The rhizome which Sir Walter and his ilk
took from the Caribbean to Europe was called *batata* from Taino. It
then became *potato*, then *Irish potato* and came back to the Caribbean
as *Irish*, the local white sweet having preempted the name *potato* or
batata in the Spanish islands. In your Caribbean kitchen its chief
virtue will not be flavour or cheapness but infinite adaptability to
whatever you have in the kitchen. At the moment fifteen papayas –
another neighbour just passed by, lovingly.

Papaya and Irish Casserole
1 large green papaya – 4 cups
2 cups Irish potato
4 raw eggs
Salt
16 slender strips cheddar cheese
or
Garlic to taste, mashed or salt

or
16 strips of pimento chopped
or
1 large onion sliced thin
1 tomato sliced thin
or
4 level teaspoons powdered onion soup
with Parmesan cheese (grated)
Leftovers to conscience
Peel, dice, steam and mash together the papaya
and the Irish.
Cooked papaya has no stamina. The Irish gives it body.
Stir in raw eggs and salt.
Put the mashed stuff in a baking casserole, and as you do, become
assertive. Crisscross the cheese strips or the pimento, or whichever of
the other ingredients you decide on.
Top with Parmesan.
The beauty of this dish is that it can be topped with any leftovers
instead of Parmesan: ham, spam, hamburger, olives, cracker crumbs,
anchovies.
After you stop being assertive, bake your decisions uncovered in low
heat until the top is brown and crusty and the aroma draws the whole
family under foot in the kitchen.

This doesn't exhaust the kaleidoscopic ingenuity of papayas, not by
many pages, but we would have to add some to the book, then the
publisher would become difficult to live with.

Let me tell you some of the horrendous things that can happen
when you grow your own bananas. Maybe you should move to a
banana island where you can buy them wholesale. I never knew they
could be so tyrannical: my bananas all ripened at once. Our gardener,
whom we dared not disobey, cut the stalk and said we had to hang it in
the house away from the birds. It must have weighed 50 lbs. They
totalled 211. There was no room in the kitchen; nor in the closet. I
tried it over my bed with the thought we might munch during the
night, but my wife heard that spiders live in bananas. It was hung over
the bathtub. The fruits ripen from the top down, in the order they
grow. I ate all I could hold. I kept slipping a banana beside my wife
while she read, until she snarled sweetly, without looking up, 'Go
marry a monkey!'

After we had boiled, baked, fried, steamed and blended our way through half the stalk, the lower levels yellowed with manic speed. They fell off into the bath. It took a lot of water to get all the squish off the enamel. We can't waste water, so I washed the neighbour's little dog, for a fringe benefit. All day she smelled like nail polish.

Here are some of the ways we disposed of the crop:

Fried Banana

Mix a syrup of brown sugar in as little water as needed. For each two tablespoons of syrup add:

$\frac{1}{2}$ teaspoon of honey

$\frac{1}{2}$ teaspoon concentrated orange juice

Slice banana lengthwise and soak in syrup for an hour, then fry lightly in butter and pour the syrup over the bananas from time to time.

Banana Stuffed Papaya

Slice a nearly ripe papaya in half lengthwise.

Remove seeds.

Mash the ripest bananas. For three bananas add:

$\frac{1}{2}$ teaspoon cream of coconut

$\frac{1}{3}$ teaspoon nutmeg

1 teaspoon rum

Stuff each papaya-half with banana mash. Dot with butter. Bake in 400° oven for about 15 minutes, less if papaya shows signs of giving up.

Fill a small bowl with rum or brandy. Light and spoon the flaming liquor on to the fruit.

Flambé bananas!

or

Chill the stuffed fruit as soon as you take it from the oven, then top with whipped cream mixed with a little honey.

Banana igloo!

Boiled Green Bananas

Native dishes often include a simple green banana (maybe two days away from full ripening) boiled and unadorned like an albino hot dog. It is good with fish stew or corned pork, or sloppy-joes with a mere mite of sweetening in the beans.

Remember when the banana industry tried to educate the radio public not to put Chiquita in the refrigerator? But if you find fifty bananas turning black – glumph in two more days – it's fridge or compost. Here's the quick solution: for every eight bananas add half a packet of cream cheese (4 oz). Mix to a liquid. Add 3 tablespoons vanilla, 4 tablespoons honey, 6 tablespoons rum. Blend well, pour into dessert cups and freeze.

The bananas and cream cheese (or thick yoghurt) form a base. You can add the juice of 1 lime, 3 tablespoons of rum with 1 tablespoon of brandy, or 4 tablespoons of Green Ginger Wine – a Caribbean favourite.

One more: to the banana cream cheese – add 4 tablespoons of carob powder, 1 tablespoon vanilla, 3 tablespoons of rum and you get an acceptable chocolate banana rum dessert, freezable.

You can do similarly with soursop. The English name is not helping this fruit's career. In the Caribbean it is travelling more widely under the Spanish alias, *guayabana* (Latin, *Annona muricata*).

The soursop is like a lovable, kind man, trapped behind a pitiably ugly face. The fruit is shaped like a very large pear that was squashed. The colour is neither green nor brown, but just a yuk. To add to the final tragedy, the poor thing is covered all over with spiky pimples.

With a face like that it has to have a superior personality. The white pulp has a delicate lemon flavour, neither sweet nor sour, yet a little of each. The glossy jet seeds are so beautifully shaped, so glistening black that they are strung into necklaces.

Mashed through a strainer to remove fibre and seeds, the soursop becomes a milky, thick juice which is diluted with water, enhanced with fresh lime and honey or sugar to produce a cool, refreshing drink.

The pulp can also be creamed, and is similar in texture to cream of coconut. It will flavour ice cream. Or you can top sponge cake soaked in orange juice. Or serve it chilled as a mystery dessert. It is not widely known.

Creamed soursop

2 cups strained pulp
$\frac{1}{2}$ cup condensed milk
$\frac{1}{4}$ cup cream of coconut
1 large or 2 small West Indian limes, juiced
$\frac{1}{3}$ cup Stones Ginger Wine
or
$\frac{1}{3}$ cup Sorrel Liqueur

$\frac{1}{4}$ cup light rum
$\frac{1}{2}$ teaspoon nutmeg
$\frac{1}{2}$ teaspoon Angostura bitters
Blend everything to a paste. Chill.
Suggestion: for the first couple of times you make this recipe, put in less than called for of everything except the soursop. You are dealing with fresh fruit and the flavour will vary. Taste from the blender and if the flavour is strong add a little more of the accessory ingredients until you achieve the mild, sweet lemony flavour of soursop in a creamy form.

The most popular use of guayabana juice, the way the canned guayabana nectar is used, is as a tall drink. Dilute the sieved pulp with water to whatever strength your taste buds approve. Enhance it with a little lime juice and honey. Before you get any ideas of enhancing it with something else, try it for a few days. Guayabana is a natural tranquillizer and many expatriates regularly slosh a few after work rather than risk the more dangerous encounter with the Caribbean's greatest evil – Old Killdevil.

There's a supposedly true story about a school board troubled by why certain children appeared stupid every morning and bright enough after lunch. Investigation showed they were from homes where guayabana juice was served for breakfast. The kids were arriving mildly smashed.

If there is anything that will rival papayas in your kitchen it is the Caribbean pumpkin.

Pumpkin soup is as classic to the islands as lobster in Maine, as fish 'n chips on the old sod. However, to recognise pumpkin soup is difficult. As first even pumpkins are difficult to recognise: green, white, striped, green and white, blotched. Sometimes you wonder what ever happened to orange? Pumpkins vary so a cook must temporise with each pot. For this reason it is a good vegetable to start your Caribbean cuisine. Never admit to making a mistake. You make a discovery. You may be working with a double-decker as though a small pumpkin were being birthed from a larger. Many are flat.

The proprietress of Virgin Gorda's renowned Olde Yard Inn, an authority on pumpkin soup, says it is virtually impossible to make exactly the same soup from day to day. So to her dashes of this and pinches of that she adds a touch of customer psychology. She

emphasises: THE INFINITE SUBTLETIES OF PUMPKIN
SOUP:

Basic Pumpkin Soup

If you start with a 3 lb chicken, you can use a 4 lb pumpkin – more but
not less. Also:

2 large onions, chopped
1 large carrot, chopped
2 stalks celery, chopped
$\frac{1}{2}$ can beef broth
2 teaspoons soy sauce
1 teaspoon marjoram
$\frac{1}{2}$ teaspoon sweet basil
2 teaspoons parsley

Optional are the traditional West Indian blenders, catalysts for all the
flavours without creating a flavour of their own. They somehow
permeate and accentuate the whole.

Use any or all of the following:

1 tablespoon cream of coconut
1 teaspoon nutmeg
3 teaspoons rum

Cut the chicken into parts and steam-stew in enough water to barely
cover. After five minutes of full steam, add the onions. When meat is
soft enough to pull off the bones throw away skin, debone and set meat
aside for a different dish. Return bones to stock.

Cut the pumpkin into hunks, with skin, about the size of a cup. Set the
pumpkins on the bones and steam until you can easily plunge in a fork
and lift the pumpkin from the pot without having the pulp fall apart.
Cool pumpkin, cut off rind. Throw away bones.

Return pumpkin with carrot and celery to stock and stew everything
until soft enough to go through blender. There should be twice as
much pulp as liquid.

Add the rest of the ingredients and optionals while blending.

Let everything have time to get well acquainted in the fridge. Heat,
and just before serving add a couple more teaspoons of rum, if you're
the type.

The Olde Yard's recipes seem to tend more to purity of taste.
Pumpkin soup tastes like Pumpkin.

Pumpkin Soup
1 10 lb pumpkin
1 large onion, coarsely sliced
1 teaspoon salt
2 cups double cream
2 teaspoons nutmeg
Extra salt and pepper to taste
A selection of garnishes: for serving hot – crumbled bacon bits or croutons: for cold – chopped onion or sour cream.
Peel and cube the pumpkin.
Boil with sliced onion and salt in enough water to cover, until tender.
Drain and retain liquid.
Put pulp through blender, add liquid to smooth.
Add cream, nutmeg, extra salt and pepper as desired.
Serve hot or cold with choice of garnishes.

Pumpkin with Nutty Sauce
Cut your pumpkin into chunks the size of small apples. Leave the skin on and steam. The skin is good to eat.
Those who appreciate the skin of a baked potato will enjoy the pumpkin rind.
Steam the pumpkin until it becomes tender but still holds together when you lift it by jabbing with a fork.
Twenty minutes starting with cold water should be enough. While it is cooking you have just time to make the sauce.

Yeast Yoghurt Sauce
6 heaped teaspoons plain yoghurt (flavoured yoghurt contains sugar, consult your dentist). If yoghurt is too runny to heap, scoop from bottom where it is firmer.
4 heaped tablespoons mayonnaise to add body to yoghurt
6 level teaspoons brewer's yeast
4 teaspoons soy sauce
1 brimming teaspoon lime juice = 1 West Indian lime
Stir vigorously until it becomes a lovely sun-tanned coloured satiny cream. Serve in a gravy boat and let guests pour over the pumpkin chunks. Those who think the flavour is somewhat like a Brazil nut will go for it. Those who know it is yeast may be likely to skimp. So don't tell them. If they do not know that uncooked yeast is one of the two richest sources of vitamin B, they are not up with the times about nutrition.

The yeast imparts a bewitching flavour to offset the rather Cinderella-ishness of plain steamed pumpkin.

However, you can use butter with a little lime juice.

Or flambé with brandy.

Or two tablespoons of sour cream and 1 teaspoon of honey.

So, having plenty of pumpkin in the house is not such a dreadful burden after all, not when it is such a versatile vegetable.

Your Caribbean kitchen cannot live as an island unto itself; it has to be influenced by the distinctiveness of Caribbean shopping.

A favourite question from visitors to the islands is: 'Say, what's it like to live all year round here?'

'Different!' That's the most blanket answer. Even to such an unsand-and-surf consideration as grocery shopping, the difference is persistence. For many items, all shops depend on the same freighter. So, when de boat don fetch, all the shops at the same time give the same answer: 'That finished.'

You write a shopping list but subconsciously think up a substitute list. Here is a sample Vichyssoise conventional recipe and a 'that finished' list. Use tania instead of Irishes which are sometimes available, only old and soggy.

Tania is a white root, most pleasantly peeled under water because it is slippery under the skin. It's related to the familiar taro and the Hawaiian poi and the elephant-ear plant of bank lobbies. This recipe is more than a sample of how to shop when de boat don fetch: it introduces tania.

'That finished' Vichyssoise
(about 6 cupfulls)

Potato Vichyssoise
3 medium sized leeks
1 medium onion
2 tablespoons butter

'That finished' version
(leeks?) try celery tops
Onions – Okay
Butter – Danish, Dutch, English
Irish, all Okay and plentiful.

Mince all vegetables together and sauté in butter until tender. Add:
4 medium sized Irishes
or
equivalent in tania
Peel and steam until soft.
Mix tania and the sautéed vegetables in 4 cups chicken broth. Strong stock makes a thicker soup, and a stronger flavour: so go heavier on the following items if using strong stock.
Put all above through the blender. Now add:
$1\frac{1}{2}$ cups cream
or
$\frac{1}{2}$ cup water plus $1\frac{1}{2}$ cups evaporated milk
Salt and pepper
Chopped watercress
or
Dried chives soaked a few hours in water.
Serve hot or cold with a 'guess what this is made of' conversation.

Now we come to the post-graduate Caribbean kitchen. A very common question is 'Where can we sample native food?' probably asked by a continental of a resident expatriate who probably won't know either. The 'native dishes' served by restaurants are modified native foods, adapted to mainland hesitancy. Truly native food is being displaced gradually by mainland convenience packages. This is especially true on islands where both man and wife work full time outside the home.

Traditionally, native cooking uses several starches in the same serving, without salad. The predominant vegetables are pumpkin, sweet potato, tania, breadfruit, plantain and green bananas, and sometimes cassava.

Pumpkins you've met (you probably still have fifteen under your sink).

The sweet potato, or batata, is the vegetable for people who think they don't like sweet potatoes. It is white with a flavour that captivates the most ardent non-sweet eater. On Statia, at the Old Canward, it was served like a slice of tomato, with nothing else – no butter, no mayonnaise. In its simplicity it was superb.

Tania you have met. Slimy when peeled, it is dry and mild when cooked. It will never make cordon bleu.

Breadfruit is versatile but difficult to find in the northern islands. It is usually stewed, a sweet yellow delicate chunk. It can be breaded, diced, baked and french fried.

Plaintain and green bananas are natively served boiled but can be transformed by frying with brown sugar and honey and butter and called a 'native' dish.

Cassava doesn't thrill mainlanders except as manioc and tapioca. The roots are sweet or bitter. The bitter contains hydro-cyanic acid and must be roasted to eliminate the poison. Don't serve it uncooked unless you are fantasising as Lucrezia Borgia.

Local meats need no comment except 'muttin'. It can be sheep mutton or goat mutton. However, sheep mutton is easier to obtain so, if you want to sample goat, request it. There is hardly any difference in flavour or texture. All the libellous remarks about goat must pertain to a mainland strain. In restaurants influenced by Puerto Rico, as on St Croix, for instance, goat may be called *cabrito*. A goat by any other name – can still be delicious.

However, the West Indian staff of life, according to all the cooks interviewed, still is fish.

Traditional native cooking is mostly stew or soup or fry. The fry differs little from mainland. The difference between stew and soup is, as explained by one local lady, that the soup spreads out more.

Soup is made by chopping the fish and boiling it. Bones are strained out. Then added to the broth are tania, sweet potato, butter, salt, pepper, macaroni and dumpling.

Dumpling deserves a paragraph to itself – later.

Stew is formed differently. The fish is seasoned. Butter, onion, spaghetti, garlic and tomato are covered with a little water. The fish is laid on top. As steam rises, it forms a gravy which drops over the vegetables. Stew doesn't 'spread out' like soup.

Perhaps the most native of native dishes, certainly one enjoyed throughout the islands, is corned pork. Pronounce it 'cawnpoke'.

Fresh pork, newly killed, is cut into strips and rubbed thinly with salt and pepper. It is hung in a large pot to drain out the blood. It drains in a day. Then it is washed in sea water and hung a day in air but not in sun.

The pork is now soaked in fresh water overnight, boiled from early morning until soft.

The final seasoning varies with the cooks. One recipe calls for cutting the pork into thin slices and cooking with sweet oil, onion and lime. Another restaurant makes a sauce of onions, hot peppers, lime

136

and vinegar in which the pork is cooked for a few minutes. It imparts a subtle undercurrent of warmth to the soft, sweet pork flavour.

And now, the dumpling. This you are not likely to encounter in any 'native dish' place. But expect it in native stews. However, native helpings are more than enough.

It is made from white flour in a bowl mixed with salt and butter. Add water, knead till smooth, shape and boil. What results is a slab or white substance of flexible firm quality that is cut into tiles. Your serving is likely to be a rectangle about two inches by four and three-eights thick. Some restaurants omit the butter; it is then less plastic. Boiled in the broth, it absorbs a flavour, slightly.

A variation is the corn meal dumpling – one part corn meal to three parts of flour.

So much for the Caribbean dumpling.

However, as we said in the beginning, your Caribbean kitchen will have no difficulty at all in getting hotel quality ribs, Boston strip, frozen asparagus . . . .

TWELVE
In the garden . . . goats

To say 'Gardening in the Caribbean' is like saying 'Gardening in Europe'. Would you start with the Côte d'Azure or the Alps? The uniform temperature over the vast area from the coast of South America to the tip of Florida tends to give gardeners the euphoria of perpetual summer – and becloud the many variations in altitude and soils and rainfall. One has the desire to make the gorgeous white lily of ginger from St Vincent bloom on the dry east end of St Thomas and with enough water why would not the anthuriums of Martinique lend brilliance to the flats of St Maarten or Anguilla? Yet the fact of gardening in the Caribbean is that there are trees thriving on Cariacou which do not grow on lush Grenada only a few miles to the south. And on Puerto Rico to the north you can find five levels of climatic variations.

Gardeners tend to be honest with each other. Let's start with reality: save the palm tree romance for house guests. All-year-round gardening in the Caribbean is wonderfully rewarding once you get the hang of drought, flood, tropical light intensity, goats, grasshoppers, and things that go chew in the night.

The even climate which is so healthy for you, insects thrive on, also. (Americans might practise saying 'insects' in this multilinguistic world. Among many of the British islanders 'bug' means 'bedbug'. Your innocent question while viewing the garden: 'Do you have many bugs?' does not promote an invitation to stay the night.)

Where Dominica has over 300 inches of rain, Virgin Gorda gets 40; where Barbados has a dry season, Puerto Rico has a rain forest; and cane-carpeted St Kitts and Eden-lush St Vincent have fresh water to sprinkle the sea; there is only one rule for the new gardener. Follow it scrupulously and you will need no other – ask a native. And remember, 'native' means someone born on that island, not anyone with brown skin. A person from the rice fields of Trinidad is not likely to be a reliable agronomist about why orange trees suddenly fall over on Anguilla, or why whole stands of papayas within days of each other go clunk on Anegada. At first with your native friends you may encounter two problems: accent – yours, and shyness – theirs. Specific, short questions will overcome both.

No matter where you plan to create your botanical garden, destined to make the Rockresorts look shabby, some widespread experiences may be useful. If your land is along a rocky coast or somewhat eroded hillside, give up any idea of planting according to a formal plan unless you have a rare plot which you know is well covered with soil. Straight rows of hedge will be most successful if you stick to cactus, especially monkey-no-climb. Trees should be artistically grouped in threes or fives – and be sure the holes are dug before planting starts. You cannot know how far under the soil is a large stone, or worse, mother rock. Local farmers speak of plants as having intelligence and a will of their own. They say of a tree, when its tap root feels a large stone, it gets discouraged and thinks the struggle useless. So it either lives as a sterile dwarf or falls over and dies.

You can plant five papayas in a row, and have numbers two and five sprout and fruit before your visa expires, while the rest act as though a snowstorm were en route. You won't know why unless you dig down just a little farther than you dug for the original hole. You may find a rock, or you may find a stem-borer just waiting for a nice stem to climb into. Your solution is to dig holes much deeper than needed merely for rooting. For this a posthole digger is efficient.

Exceptions to the deep hole are three trees found throughout the Caribbean, all of them valuable as cost-cutters for your food budget: sugar apples, soursops and papaya. Seeds dropped into a trench a couple of inches deep, if watered, should become trees. They spread shallow roots. Papayas are absurdly easy to plant from seed. Never use seed of papaya – or any other plant – which has been refrigerated and use only the ripest, blackest seed. Scratch the ground. Throw in a dozen seeds, then weed out eleven of the sprouts. Papaya roots spread so shallowly the plants often are blown over. A precaution is to deepen the soil over the roots as the plant grows taller.

The soursop tree can grow to thirty feet and is thick and well shaped. It can be used as an ornamental tree but should not be located nearer the house than you would plant a maple.

The sugar apple, also called sweetsop, is a lot shorter, often more like a large bush. It is deciduous. It is less dense and less decorative.

The papaya looks tropical. As a silhouette it goes with the coconut and like the coconut it loses leaves as it grows. In three years it can get to be just a top on a skinny stalk unless it can put out side stalks. It changes so fast that it is not good in a planned, decorative garden, but is probably number one as a fruit tree. If you want to include papaya in a decorative garden, plant a low growing shrub about three feet on each side, for instance hibiscus, jasmine or lantana.

The sugar apple is excellent as a snack, a dessert or as a juice to sweeten other fruits. The soursop, more favourably known as guayabana, gets a rave notice in Kadans' *Encyclopedia* of fruits, vegetables, nuts and seeds. It contains almost all vitamins, minerals, carbohydrates and some fat, protein and calories. Kadans considers it almost a complete food and suggests it for slimming. (You might like to have on hand a copy of Kadans' *Encyclopedia*, printed by Parker Publishing Company, West Nyack. N.Y.). The papaya is such a fundamental part of the tropical diet that it will get full treatment farther along.

The West Indian lime grows anywhere, is thoroughly satisfactory, and so full of vitamin C that it belongs in the medicine chest.

The bitter and basic fact of gardening in the Caribbean isles, which are not shaded by thick overhead foliage, is that the ground bakes to five inches in August, the killer month. Plants which do not have their roots well below five inches will die in August. Therefore, you need enough water to soak to five inches occasionally between the last saturating rain in spring or summer and the first saturating rain in autumn.

The drip pipe watering system was introduced a few years ago and has proved a saviour. So many expatriates leave their islands during mid-summer that the drip system has enjoyed a small boom among them. You can feel slightly depressed if after a long holiday you find all your one- and two-year-olds dead upon arrival, yours. This is the tearful voice of experience – 180 plants about eighteen years ago while I was still in the throes of palm tree fever.

The safest time to plant, for most of the Caribbean, the 'dry' islands anyway, is early September. You can expect adequate rain through November and perhaps a little in December. Then you have cool weather until spring. April and May usually bring adequate rain, but after that you need to pray for a few near misses by tropical depressions forming up into summer hurricanes on their way to the Gulf of Mexico – or put in a drip system. Plants well started in early September can make it through August of a normal year (of which there seem to be none).

If your island has only 40 to 50 inches of rain promised on a non-guaranteed basis it is as well to learn rain dancing for July during the first year of such shrubs as hibiscus and gardenia and for two years for fruit trees and such bibulous shrubs as crotons and yellow allamanda. All this arid speculation is for the Virgins, Anguilla, the Dutch islands and the Grenadines. For the remainder, except for Barbados during Christmas to Easter, water is less of a problem.

If your site is on a hillside and you want to convert from bush to flowering shrub, terrace it, even at the cost of many flowerless months. But if you contract for the bulldozer to make basic cuts what you will get is vertical ridges of top soil with horizontal planting levels of merciless subsoil. Bulldozing does not make good terracing. Dry walls are inexpensive. Actually, they adapt what nature does. Nature rolls the rocks downhill until they catch, then washes down soil to pile up behind. A dry wall works on the same principle. It slows the run-off of the rain. You can't start too soon to terrace. This is work that can be done by local youngsters even before the foundation is begun. But only an experienced gardener should build the wall. A dry wall is not a pile of stones. At best it is a double wall of large stones sandwiching a filling of small stones and rubble. The centre tends to fill tight with washed earth. It deflects wind and retains water. The double wall is more goat resistant than a single wall of stones. Where you have large rocks jutting out from the hillside several feet apart, a dry wall is a natural dam between them. Then, as Nature likes to plant trees just below the large rocks because they hold moisture under them, you can plant immediately below the dry wall.

If you don't install a drip system, build in a double valve switch-off section so that you can use grey water or sweet water. In the long run, you are far better off by completing these details, such as the double valve for the two cisterns, even though you do not plan the grey water cistern at first. You save money and fussing and, most of all, avoid the frustrations of trying later to find someone who knows what you want.

Meanwhile, get as many plants started in expendable plastic pots as you can. Store them in the shade of the construction shack and devise a hose attachment from the men's water supply for concrete.

Resist temptation to set your plants out until they are thoroughly root-bound. This is contrary to continental ways. The temptation becomes finger-twisting. A two-year-old root-bound plant, however, set into a saturated soil in September has the best chance of surviving. Again, contrary to 'old country' practice, do not water the potted plant before setting out. If the plant is in clay soil, the soil will crumble when wet. But if it is thoroughly dried, the soil will hold the shape of the pot. A long knife run around inside the pot will loosen everything yet keep the shape. However, if the cutting was raised in soft mix – peat moss and sand and anything else – the operation is this: set the pot in a bucket of water and repeatedly shake the bucket and plant until all the mix has been shed from the roots. Hold the plant in the hole and pour in water slowly while someone else shakes the live soil to fill the hole. It is like sprinkling corn starch into hot water. Now the root hairs, which you salvaged by the shaking under water in the bucket, will be gently set in moist soil.

The dry ball method is to fill the hole with water and set the dry ball in to soak for a few minutes, then displace the unabsorbed water by pouring in soft soil.

If you are where the ground will remain moist for months, you can use the hole as a potting basin. Set the cutting in the centre and lightly fill the hole, to within an inch of the rim, with potting soil, peat moss, sand and humus, having dipped the wetted end of the cutting in rooting hormone. If you keep cuttings moist for several weeks, they will continue in place. This works well for all oleanders, gardenias, turpentine trees and others that propagate easily from cuttings. But for bougainvillaea and other bad-tempered infants, it is better to start cuttings in pots, at least three for every one you need. Otherwise you will have a lot of blank spaces to fill. The pots give you a no-miss start, by providing extras of uniform age. Incidentally, plastic pots permit you to set a difficult plant in the hole then cut away the pot with a knife, even after the hole has been refilled.

Most plants that survive at all in the Caribbean can take the sun intensity, which even in the northern countries such as Hispaniola and the Virgins, is lethally more than Florida. For young plants and some vegetables, you will need to provide screening nets. In fact, all cuttings benefit from shade for their first months.

The sea blast, however, is not so easily counteracted. Many plants and trees that will thrive two hundred feet back from the beach will not thrive at one hundred. Salt spray is the killer. A hedge can be made from haiti-haiti (tree hibiscus), sea grape, pitchapple – and consult your local mermaids for anything special on your island.

Parkinsonia, yellow elder and luckynut make beautiful wind-breakers, the parkinsonia and yellow elder having the advantage of being feathery so they do not give the impression of a barrier so much as a veil. They can be skilfully used to create a wind-screen between you and your view without obscuring it, yet make a windshield for more tender plants downwind of them. They all bloom.

Yellow elder could not be easier to start, and, goats willing, they are hardy. Their bloom is not continuous, but they combine with several other blooming trees so that their blooming periods come as an emphasis to all the others. You can plant seed in place any time if you are prepared to water a little for any dry spell. Prepare the ground as you would for a northern seed bed, flat and fine. Sprinkle the seeds, which you can gather by the thousands from wherever you come across a tree. Sprinkle as you would pepper on a tasteless steak. Cover lightly with fine soil and keep moist until the second leaves show. Then weed out until the best stand five feet apart. These can be kept trimmed to a three foot hedge. If you then plant parkinsonia three feet back from the hedge, you will have a curtain of gold almost all year, from the ground up.

Cashew trees grow throughout the Caribbean. They provide an apple (similar in appearance and flavour to persimmon), a nut (poisonous until roasted), and an evergreen tree of compact spheroid beauty.

Some plants are fussy about being depotted. Cashews are fussy.

They are wonderfully hardy and drought resistant after they are set so the trick is not to let them know they are being kicked out of bed. For these crankies dig a hole about two and a half widths of the pot. Slightly mound a cushion of soil at the bottom of the hole. Cut the bottom off the pot, carefully, not slashing the roots. Press the pot on to the cushion to eliminate air. Now cut the pot from bottom to rim in thirds. Be careful not to cut into roots. Leave just enough pot at the top rim to hold it together while you fill the hole with water and add soil to about an inch and a half of the rim. Now you can water inside the pot top and have the water sweep down to encourage the roots to spread out deep below the baking surface of the earth. About four months later finish cutting the rim and remove the three side panels.

Always leave the earth around a plant in depression so you can puddle water.

The following plants are in bloom almost all year round and are less likely to break your heart than some others you might try after you are better acquainted with wind, sea blast, soil, drought and grasshoppers: oleander, hibiscus, ginger lilies (St Vincent region), ixora, heliconia (Barbados area), allamanda vine (big flower) and shrub (little flower – fragrant). With these you get a vast variety of coloured leaf crotons but they do need water.

The following trees and shrubs grow easily: hibiscus, oleander, bougainvillaea (but difficult to make cuttings), poor-man's orchid, sea-grape, haiti-haiti, frangipani (wild and hybrid), flamboyant and Pride of Barbados – a dwarf flamboyant extremely easy to grow from seed, in several colours. Poinsettias were once a Mexican weed. Start some in pots for December to March colour. Then set them out. But watch out, if they like the locations, they can shoot up twenty feet.

Fruit trees to try in addition to sugar apples, papaya, and soursop: mescales (from Jamaica, fruit in two to three years); grafted juli mango (if it tastes like turpentine, it's not juli). The dwarf mango needs a special soil mix but – no big 'ting. Lime likes the same soil mix but does beautifully planted near or between large rocks. There's a Caribbean plum – if you have the extra room.

The following comment comes from one of the north Caribbean's largest agricultural stations: 'Pineapples are easy to grow. (The station gets government support.) Be sure you have a fresh fruit, not from a supermarket where it has probably been chilled. Wearing a glove, twist out the core. You will have the crown of leaves with the point of core meat attached. It needs no water and tolerates poor soil.'

144

Then you wait.

Eventually maybe you'll move to Puerto Rico where they can the things.

Eating bananas, avocados (known locally only as pears), and all citrus trees need water. That's why St Lucia and its neighbours are known as banana islands. If you choose to live in that region, one of the never-ending delights will be the big white banana boats loading.

For the less-than-a-truck-load grower the custom is to plant bananas in the flow of the septic tank effluent. Flamboyants planted near the septic tank will astonish you with their fast growth. Later you can be astonished again by the roots cracking the tank. Bananas don't do anything nasty, but they are very, very, very intolerant of other roots, especially grasses.

The following plants need little water and tolerate poor soil: mango, dwarf coconut, fig banana, plantain, pineapple (they say in the agricultural station); horse and donkey bananas, which are larger than the fig banana, do better near the septic effluent. Some homes run the shower water off into a space separate from the septic effluent, just for bananas. Papayas grow anywhere except on top of a stone.

Papayas are probably the most encouraging plant for newcomers. But they are fussy like cashews about being transplanted, though there is no need to do it, since the seeds sprout anywhere.

They are used as a vegetable while in white meat, similar to summer squash. Pink, they are also cooked, often mixed with Irish or sweet potatoes which add body to the soft papaya. They can be candied, preserved, juiced, jellied and made into ice cream. Tough but tasty meat can be sliced thin and placed between fresh papaya leaves, weighted with a plate and left in the refrigerator overnight. In the morning – you have beef tenderloin tips. Papaya contains a tenderising agent throughout the plant, most conveniently obtained from the leaves or mashed seed. If you score a green papaya with short knife cuts, or, as a guest-house hostess on Statia explained, 'Give he some liddle jabs', the papain will leak from the skin and in a few days the flesh will ripen and the skin turn yellow but the flavour will not be as lucious as a tree ripened fruit.

Depending upon the rain you can enjoy fruit from a seedling in fifteen to twenty months. The plant should fruit well for up to twenty years. Uncontrolled, they tend to become too tall for picking and scrawny to look at. When the plant is about six feet high the top can be chopped off with a cutlass in two strokes leaving a V head. Each stem of the V will grow into a more horizontal branch, making the plant easier to harvest and of a more bushy silhouette. You can chop the head into two Vs, pointing in four directions. Then you get four branches, which will be, however, weaker and as they grow longer may require propping up.

The papaya is the most flagrantly sexist plant in the Caribbean, even outdoing the anthurium. The female produces a yellow cuplike blossom directly on the main stalk. When this is fertilised, it closes into a womblike casing within which the fruit develops and grows eventually into a melon-like pendant still directly attached to the main stalk.

The male plant produces a long pendulum covered with short clusters of yellow flowers full of pollen. The tiny male blossoms are designed to offer pollen, nothing more.

It is generally agreed that fruit which has been male fertilised is better, but if no plants are available the females can become hermaphroditic. Unfortunately, there is no way of knowing the sex of papaya until it is too late to do anything about it. However, to Mother Nature, being such a female chauvinist, males are expendable. You can pull up excess males and plant more seed. Or you can experiment for the fun of it. Take the top of a male and twist off the whole top of the tree. Or top the plant V-style. The male thus treated sometimes turns female: a sort of transexual surgery among the fruits. Local neighbours will offer other nostrums such as dropping a stone down the hollow stalk or driving an iron nail into the stalk, which may be chemically justified. Twisting off the top is the only process I can vouch for. A storm performed the operation on St Thomas, success-fully. Incidentally, when you weed out, leave one good male upwind; he will take care of his whole harem. How Nature does enjoy repeating a clever idea: I remember reading in a medical book that one healthy human male produces enough seed to repopulate the whole city of New York – every time the wind blows.

The stalk of the large papaya plant is a hollow pipe. The natives of the Carolina region, before the arrival of Europeans, used to drive a papaya trunk into moist soil and create a well.

Papayas become a tree you love. They can also break your heart, because sometimes they just fall over, for no apparent reason. If this happens to you, have the soil checked for nematodes, worms so minute they are not apparent. The only fact I know about nematodes comes from research in progress on Anegada, BVI. They live in barren soil. Once the ground becomes fertilised, they go away. To date, the handiest solution is to invite a herd of cows to take a holiday on your land.

One of your privileges in the Caribbean will be to surround your house with year-round fragrance. The tall deep pink oleander is fragrant. Put it upwind and far away from the house because, full grown, it can shut off the air. The hybrid frangipani adorns any garden, but does not bloom all year. Also, it is deciduous. The short yellow allamanda can be planted around the frangipani. They do need water to bloom. The islands, especially the 'down islands' are redolent with jasmines. There is the Lady-of-the-day, a cultivated plant, naturally. Lady-of-the-night grows wild. She blooms for long periods, twice a year. Since you will have windows open day and night all year long, planning your perpetual fragrance should get as much priority as planning your driveway.

Anywhere in the shade of your house, put gardenias. They make a handsome dark bush and can grow ten feet tall. They hate wind. They like shade. They insist on plenty to drink. Then how they do put out! You can make several cuttings from one branch. They grow nicely in medium-sized pots so you can have them in your patio or courtyard while you are waiting for the regulars to come up, then move them around the house wherever there is temporary need.

While we are being ecstatic over jasmine and such, let us do a quick swing in the opposite direction: hibiscus is to goats as catnip is to cats. If there is a goat around – and where are there not goats around? – you will need to fence your property or enclose hibiscus with stakes and chicken wire until the shrubs are well matured, about three feet tall. Then they can survive an occasional stripping off of all their leaves. Goats do not bite stems. They sort of suck the leaves off. Of course, sometimes stems break or small plants are uprooted.

If you elect to fence, the best public relations time to do it is while the workmen have your grounds in a total mess. If you put it up later it will look like a very un-West Indian act of exclusivity. Put the fence a full foot inside your boundary and plant immediately the low, pale oleander. The shrub will quickly bush out and up to hide the fence. No problem at all – also, no mar on your landscape. It's an enhancement, in fact.

Hibiscus can be grown well in tubs which can be moved around like gardenias for the first year or so and then set out after the fence is established.

Back to the snake in Eden: during drought, goats in search of water will eat nearly any plant they do not ordinarily sample. They never touch oleander. What is so provocative about goats is that all goats, even the youngest, know oleander is poisonous, yet many humans do not.

Now you see the depth of wisdom behind your fence cum oleander? A relatively low, inexpensive but strong chainlink fence covered with oleander will keep goats out without offending your neighbours.

Goats are ubiquitous and intelligent so we may as well face up to them now. They do not mind visiting a house and will peer through a glass door to see who is home and how well occupied the tenant is. Goats can and do tiptoe into gardens at night and strip off all vegetables, grape leaves and other gourmet delights.

Just what the law regarding goats is on all islands, I do not know. But this is important beyond a goat; the law is similar because it antedates the influx of expatriates, and antedates the present form of island government. It is enforced largely by public acceptance. Therefore, it is actually a custom dealing with a sensitive situation. In the US Virgins, population density has triumphed over goatery. In the British Virgins the law is that a homeowner may shoot a goat trespassing on his property. He must cut off the head and lay it in the street. He keeps the carcass, for the owner to claim, as long as he can. Then he disposes of it. He must not eat it. That makes him a hunter and the whole deal is changed.

That's the law. The custom-laws are similar throughout the area. Jump over to St Vincent and you get an added fillip: if the invading goat has a rope or chain around its neck, evidence that the owner tried, you return it to the owner and claim damages. No rope? Off with his head!

Now the practice. If you hurt a goat, the owner will claim compensation. If a goat hurts your property, it is wild – an unwritten law of the Caribbean.

Good neighbours tether their goats on a hill-side to graze each day. One of the pastoral delights of living anywhere here is the little herds being taken out for staking each morning and led home at dusk by youthful goatherds: youthful? Sometimes they are barely more than toddlers.

Not all owners are conscientious about tethering. So then your procedure is to estimate the damage; just as all damaged goats become pedigreed, all your hibiscus can become hybrid and professionally grown. You put a notice with estimate of damage in the local paper, or lacking a newspaper, you tack the notice on the nearest Announcement Tree. You ask the owner to compensate or you will have to shoot the goat.

Naturally, no one will come forward but you will have taken the first step toward claiming the goats are wild.

Step two is to request a shotgun licence. Here's where you learn some more about your island. For example, an American in the US Virgins need only register a handgun with the police to possess it legally. In the British Virgins, anyone not a native (Belonger) is forbidden to possess any fire-arm except a shotgun, specifically for killing goats. You obtain a licence from the chief of police. Check into the gun law on the down-islands. There's a lot of difference, especially around St Kitts/Nevis.

While this suppressed goat violence is on bubbling, you can quietly follow the advice of the St Thomas Agricultural Station. Spray your hibiscus and other attractive plants with malathion. This makes goats ill. Because they are such intelligent creatures with some sort of excellent communication system, they will pass the word that such and such a garden is using bad merchandise.

The legal process of decapitation may sound unsporting, unAmerican, unBritish or just nauseating. However, from time to time on the street you see evidence that the custom is accepted and effective. Just think of it as part of the European royal heritage: the kings used to impale heads of annoying citizens along the roadside.

On most of the islands that are being preferred by expatriates, your first true gardening act should be done to do homage to the few trees. During the Great Depression on the northern islands, notably in the Virgins, all trees which did not bear fruit and still would make good charcoal were coaled. The 'coal' was sold to Puerto Rico for cooking fuel, the islanders' only cash crop. Fortunately, loblolly and turpentine trees do not make good coal. On the wetter islands the trees went to make room for cotton or sugar. Sometimes an island suffered a unique form of deforestation. On St Croix, once a garden of towering hardwoods, the early settlers set fire to the island upwind, got in their boats and waited until the island was burnt out. The idea was to drive off the 'humours'. Here and there on St Croix, St Thomas and Tortola you can see stands of huge and noble trees that tell of a future that was destroyed. So now it is up to you – plant trees and help preserve the earth's supply of oxygen for breathing. It's a little bit necessary.

If your parcel has trees, you will surely locate your house to save those precious relics. If you have brush, it will need to be 'brushed out'. Brushing out is different from mainland 'clearing off'. Brushing out consists of removing the lower branches from trees with trunks three-quarters of an inch or more. This makes the plant grow taller to shade the ground yet permits you to see under and remove whatever is left on the ground.

Too often the eager-to-get-it-done-right-away new landowner arrives with his chainsaw and sets his example of how it should be done, the way he did it back home. If you 'clear off', as though you were expecting some McCormick equipment, you will have flayed earth. The sun will scorch it. Nothing will survive until rain brings a grass cover. Your damage may be repaired in another five years or so.

It is best to hire a native to do the brushing out. The work is tedious and needs someone who will study the top branches of each stripling to be saved.

You should let the trash trees become parasols. Plant seedlings in their shade. Two years later cut down the parasols.

Once your land is brushed out, you can plant a variety of ground covers to hold the moisture and soil until you get around to the long-term planting. Pumpkins, watermelons and Caribbean potatoes make ground cover vines. Pumpkins are a popular and versatile vegetable given better treatment in Chapter Eleven. As ground cover they are erratic. Watermelons are steady cover but the fruit is problematical. From island to island you hear variations of failure. Usually the West Indian melon is pale, uninviting, less tasty but nevertheless enjoyed by local people for the juice. Some say the northern seeds produce poorly because of light intensity. Therefore they are experimenting by growing melons in shade. The most successful experiment I have tasted was from a vine sprayed regularly for spider mite. The spiders under the leaves cause the leaves to wither. Therefore, the fruit does not get all its nutrition. When the leaves were preserved, without extra water and in full sun, the vine produced fruit every bit as Georgian or New Jersian, although smaller. The experiment continues. Potatoes are such pets in the Caribbean (local sweet whites) that one tends to forgive the periodic nature of their ground cover. Of course, as you dig up the hills, the cover is disturbed.

Flowering ground cover, considered for cover only, is superior. Wadelia spreads well and thickly and is satisfactory except during prolonged drought. It comes back but, during the drought, when you want it most, it isn't there. Sutter's Gold is thicker, quicker and slightly more drought resistant. It also comes back if it does have to retreat for a while. Most consistent of all is a feathery succulent called in the Virgins 'Evergreen', not found in flower books. If all else fails have a friend in the BVI give you a few sprigs. It spreads well.

Whatever you use, never remove fallen leaves. Natural mulch is a treasure here. You can improve your ground by adding a **Never-again** to your list – Never again rake leaves! Once your garden matures and the shrubs spread in all directions, your ground mulch becomes a pleasure to walk on. Also it breeds beetles and beetles attract lizards and lizards bring good luck. You can't beat that for positive thinking.

Pigeon peas can be planted for a quick, feathery hedge. They grow fast to five or six feet, producing small yellow flowers and an almost continuous crop. They are what is usually mixed with rice in Spanish cooking. When one row is in flower you can plant the next. If the plant becomes straggly after a crop you whack it back and it will branch out. It is not an ornamental, but is useful as a temporary ornamental. For example, you can plant pigeon peas outside your fence for quick cover while you wait for the oleander cuttings to become pot bound. Your neighbours will enjoy picking the free dinner.

Aloe is the Aloe Vera of $15/oz. cosmetics. Cadge a few roots from wherever. Plant them unceremoniously – on any bald spot. They spread. Peel a leaf. The green gunk that oozes out is excellent for all kinds of burns, itches and whatyoumaycallits of the skin.

Small islands are likely to be lacking in magnesium. Strange, being so near the sea, but magnesium deficiency seems characteristic of littorals. Beaches provide endless amounts of seaweed, rich in all the sea salts. Be sure the ocean salt is well washed off by rain. Nothing is a better mulch or humus maker than seaweed.

After you have your kitchen, you can put all organic waste through your blender. Unless you want to compost, you can use this rich fluid in either of two ways:

1 With a post hole digger, sink shaft two feet deep around shrubs. Pour the potage de peelings avec eggshells into the hole and top lightly with a dressing of fine soil – enough to discourage fruit flies. When the hole is filled to about five inches of the surface, top off with soil. If you are sceptical, check back in six months. The hole will be full of rootlings, feasting themselves into a fat tangle.

2 Toss the blender mix directly on to the earth. This is the way

151

Mother Nature handles fallings en route to becoming mulch. After one day of our sun – instant humus. The dried blender-mixed humus should be scratched into the soil every few days or it might attract night creatures. This is actually an accelerated composting.

A word of caution for you who might buy near or actually in wooded areas. There are several poisonous plants generally known as Cow-itch, an example of how the West Indians like all words to have clear, quick meanings. The dictionary doesn't help. Some purists insist it is cowage. Anyway – touch them and they cause skin blisters. Asking a native to identify them is of little help. You can pick a branch and ask if it is poisonous. He may laugh and say that since he a boy he eat that. The next morning your hand may be covered with little blisters. The Caribbean holly is certainly one. Its tiny leaves are surrounded with spikes, each of which stings and poisons. Generally, you can feel the sting or the itch starting. I have found, after years of experimenting, a reliable cure. Wear long pants and sleeves. When you do get hit, wash thoroughly as soon as you can. Then smear the washed area with Betadine. Let it dry and read a book or stare out the window for about four minutes. Then wash thoroughly with an antiseptic soap (a supply is often available at mom-and-pop stores). There is also a blue soap and one called *antiseptic*. You should have no problems thereafter.

Another home-grown idea is to take a fifty gallon drum, or the equivalent, to catch the overflow from your cistern. You will probably feel so jubilant that the cistern is finally full you may want to save the first quart, something like holy water. But most cisterns overflow a couple of times a year. The drum becomes a source of daily watering for transplants. Mark the drum inside in feet for measurement of water depth. It will also measure the amount of water you are using and the amounts you gain from rains which more than fill your cistern. If the drum becomes a mosquito nursery, put a few drops of vegetable oil on the water, enough to coat the surface, and suffocate the wigglers. Don't use petroleum oil. It's poisonous to plants.

However, if you decide to live on St Vincent, Puerto Rico, St Kitts or St Lucia, please don't smirk at all this talk about water. Rejoice that St Vincent has only a dry March, and Barbados only a dry January and February, and Puerto Rico only a dry underside. Those who pick dry islands can boast about eternal sunshine (almost).

For those who will have to learn to live with a fluctuating water supply, a simple scheme may help at the beginning. Plant, far away from the house, only those plants which can survive a drought. You may have one the first year. Plant near the house anything that will want a lot of water. Plant many flowering things in pots and tubs to have close to the house, on the deck, patio and courtyard so that you can have instant joy in your new home. Start the cuttings and trays of seedlings just as soon as you are sure you can water them. If you plan to be away for several months, put in a drip system, even if you are lucky enough to hire a gardener, because any islanders live in dread of water shortage; they just cannot bring themselves to water deeply. If you have large rocks, capitalise on them. Build on to them or, if they are in the garden, emphasise them with orchids and philodendra.

Our gardening thoughts have skipped from water conservation, to goat decapitation, to how to depot crankies. These are some of the things that confront you immediately in Caribbean gardening. Soon afterwards many continentals become achingly aware of their boundaries, as though they were still living where one sixty foot lot infringed on another if the owner so much as looked across. But afterwards there comes the burgeoning urge to own everything. It is a race to see how many types of hibiscus, and how many colours of bougainvillaea you can produce.

Meanwhile, the garden just keeps on growing, without stops for death by cold. Gradually the realisation of Caribbean bountifulness seeps into you and you're tempted to supplement it with just a few lovelies from back home. Of course they die and you feel angry with them: why shouldn't a lousy little nasturtium be honoured to live in such ideal climate! Perhaps this is when you try to compensate, with something your neighbours do not have – perhaps one of those huge dangling ferns from the heights of Saba, or a pink poui like an earthbound cloud from Trinidad. This will satisfy you, you tell yourself. But they get homesick.

So you keep adding and adding and the garden keeps changing and changing, yet somehow year after year it manages to come back to the same survivors. Only, each year there is so much more of them and they are so healthy!

Gradually you begin to fall in love – all around. Perhaps it's a brazenly spectacular flamboyant that overhangs the road a little way from you. You await the sweet envelopment from your neighbour's jasmine. Each night it mingles with the scent from your gardenias that blows down upon your neighbour.

All the flowers live out of doors. The people live out of doors with them, theirs and yours.

You are where no tall buildings imprison your sight; where the ordinary shopping trip leads you beside the sea; where a distant old loblolly on a hill suddenly bursts into flames of pink because a Mexican creeper has reached its top. You begin your garden beyond your boundaries. All around you the whole island drips with blossom and all you can see are yours – to love, to smell, to be thankful for – all the year long.

After a while you learn to depend on Nature to take care of those bald spots inside your boundaries. She plants a wide frangipani, so sweet smelling. Your neighbour's yellow elder showers an old rock-pile with gold.

In time, you learn what everybody in the Caribbean learns about a garden – that everything you can see is yours and everywhere you can see is beauty. All yours.

This chapter is intended only as a taste. You will need a book on local gardening.

The National Park of St John offers a book, *A Guide to the Natural History of St John*, by Doris Jadan, P.O.Box 84, Cruz Bay, US Virgin Islands, 00830. It costs $6.00 mailed first class and has the longest list of trees and plants, plus details of sugar mills, all wrapped in admirable love of the area. For additional information write to:
University of the West Indies,
with campuses on Barbados, Jamaica
and Trinidad.

Agricultural Handbook No. 249
USDA Forestry Service
Washington, DC 20250
USA

US Department of Agriculture
Agricultural Research Service
Crops Research Division
or

154

Soil and Water Conservation Research Division,
Beltsville, Maryland 20705
USA

University of Puerto Rico
Agricultural Extension Station
Rio Piedras, Puerto Rico 00928
(*Pero amigo, aqui no se habla ingles*)

THIRTEEN
As time goes by

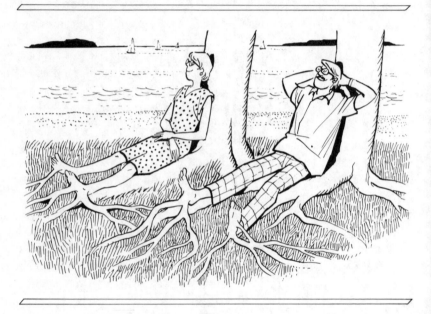

Living in the Caribbean matures in phases.

At first — wondrous Paradise — you made it! You wake and the ocean is still there, the palms, all the pizzazz just as the advertisements say. Paradise it can be, but that is an advertising claim, true at $50 to $200 a day. That kind of paradise ends whenever the wallet is flat. Hotel paradise is a man-made figment. A full life is not paradise. It is real. It does not end in two or three weeks. It goes on but always changing.

Slowly the centuries-old undercurrents of the Caribbean seep into your outlook, your sense of time, your judgement of what is important. You move by stages into a more challenging way of life, more wholesome, more lasting, if you wish it to be. The Caribbean provides an environment for your ultimate fulfillment in a nurturing climate, an atmosphere of ever-changing beauty, piqued by cultures of the world. Yet, although the Caribbean life is not critical of outsiders, it is not overly permissive. You have to earn entrée to its rich depths.

I remember saying, with all the hoary pomposity of two years in the islands, 'The Caribbean is a tiny island with massive frustrations. It's just a nicer place to be frustrated in, that's all.' I still expected the telephone to work and the shops to have just what I wanted, when I wanted it. Those who had scratched below the surface warned me merchants have a sense of who is going to stay and who will blow away. They see so many that they wait two years before learning your name.

So it was. After two years they would study my eyes as though they had never noticed before that I had any. Then, 'You on long holiday? I see you often.' Or, 'You livin' here now?' Next time, they would call me by name. I felt something but in those days I did not know what. I was entering a new phase.

Gradually, you become less critical. When there's a right French way and a right Spanish way and a right American way, there isn't a right your way. You get to thinking everybody doin' the best he can. Even if it's not true, it's a more comfortable feeling to have about people.

You become less frenetic. Your time sense changes. When you can't keep track of the days and you're never quite sure whether it's today or is it already tomorrow, and nobody near you is sure either, well, today doesn't matter too much because maybe it's already tomorrow and too late to fuss.

You gradually develop a different sense of security. The psychiatrists advise that the best way to stop worrying is to imagine what is the worst that could happen. You know it won't snow. You won't be cold. There are always more papayas and coconuts than you can eat. Taxes are so low – even the worst would take care of those. You feel closer to the essentials of life. Besides, no one else is worrying hard. Go for a swim bath.

The islands offer civilisation without mechanisation. All manufactured things produce waste. Even nature's products produce waste. But it is biodegradable waste – not toxic effluents or noxious gases. The products of the islands are fruits and games and quiet places to live leisurely. The Caribbean wastes do not pollute your life. The world already has five billion people and is threatening to double that within twenty years. The islands will become more heavily populated too. Mainland cities will continue to spread into each other along miles of roads, lined with little buildings looking alike. When you leave your neighbourhood you drive through others that look like yours: buildings, poles, signs; jam packed.

Whenever you leave an island, you sail out into the boundless sea or soar into the infinite sky, even if you are just off to Martinique or Puerto Rico for a day of shopping.

There will always be space. Your spirit can expand. There is nothing between you and the Beginning. After a while you do get used to it, but it is always there, too big to be ignored, a tonic, a cleansing of the mind flushed of its daily dribbles by the scope and calm and eternity and the closeness of the sea and the heavens.

Some people come here and hate it. They resist the island people and it gets lonely out there in space. The island population is stable. It is not for them to change. They seem to play with and watch with knowing calm whatever wave of strangers this decade's ebb and flow will toss on to their shores. The Caribbean peoples have had three centuries practice in absorbing outsiders, examining them, then ingesting or rejecting.

Some strangers think that they do the rejecting. They leave the Caribbean in a fluff of disparagement, when the truth is they were rejected before they knew it. They were squeezed out. They leave saying whatever excuse they have for their failure but the truth comes out when they claim the people aren't friendly. The fact is that islanders are expert at being absolutely frosty.

Some people seem to go all their island life loving the casinos, the boating, the beach bars. They are pleased in that they have found Paradise. But for others that life palls. For them, the better future is to open their pores, let the virtues of the Caribbean seep in, like lithium at a spar, hardly noticed.

One injection was slipped into my blood stream when my taxi to the airport broke down on top of a ridge. The driver poked it persuasively. So did passing friends. I sat on a rock to fume with my back to them. I was to have dinner that night in Philadelphia where the Canadian members of the family would bump cheeks with the Americans.

Four hundred feet below me the North Sound looked maddeningly indifferent to my turmoil. A flock of pelicans were putting on a diving show. The water was stained with an enormous patch of deeper blue. All sprats! There must have been millions of sprats. I never guessed there could be so many. No pelican could miss. They hardly bothered to rise up to take another gulp.

Suddenly six little boats veered off course, bearing down from all directions on to a man in a skiff waving his shirt. Sure enough, he was drifting towards the rocks. He wasn't more than twelve feet off a spuming jagged outcrop.

One of the six got a line tossed to him. The tow started. The line snapped. A second boat whipped into place. His line seemed to hold.

Part of me was engrossed with the rescue. Part was becoming reconciled to staying the night in San Juan and joining my family at breakfast. That didn't seem too catastrophic – certainly not as bad as a boat wreck.

The tow line held, yet the five other boats still hung around. I thought how nice boat people are. They won't be late for wherever they were going: they just won't get there as early.

The driver was waving to me, but not vigorously. The towline had his attention, also.

At the airport the plane was waiting for me. Other passengers had been late, too. Besides, the island grapevine had already told them we were only a few minutes away.

At San Juan, Eastern was late. I had dinner with the family in Philadelphia. None noticed I was an hour and a half off schedule.

I looked back at my fuming. I unknotted the stomach I suffered all the way to San Juan. Then something snapped in my inner clock. I've had a broken mainspring ever since.

That was the beginning of the end of my arthritis.

Many people move to the Caribbean to alleviate arthritis through swimming and warmth. They should add – through the way of life.

Of all the guessed-at causes for arthritis no official emphasis is placed on anxiety. Yet among the growing fraternity who now casually say, 'I used to have arthritis but not any more', anxiety is known to cause flare-ups. There is no proof that the original flare-up was not from anxiety. Anxiety creates stress and it is not necessary to add more words about what stress does to our bodies.

The time sense of the Caribbean is absolutely a specific against stress. The ambience is as well. Blessedly, island newspapers have too few pages to wallow in the horrors and incomprehensibilities of the whole world. Elections in the neighbouring islands and maybe a local accident are all that can be spared from the articles on how to raise better pumpkins or the latest grant-in-aid for extending the roads. Thank God the radio has so much static it blots out even the BBC much of the time.

The conquest of anxiety is slow, slow, slow. But the onset of arthritis was slow also. As our degenerative diseases build up over the years, they must be built down over the years. It does seem that in the Caribbean the rate of recovery is relatively fast. There are a lot of influences going for you here. Few West Indians smoke. True, smoking is increasing among the young; however, the increase is coming from a base of about zero. Then, the emphasis on swimming and sailing and do-it-yourself repairs is healthful. The air is a joy rather than a poison. The abundance of free or low cost fruits gradually weans you away from the white flour and sugar addictions. But only if you want to be weaned.

Have no doubt, you can spend your entire retirement in the glamour of casinos, and never see a sunrise. Even the tiniest islands will provide you with the world's best processed convenience foods. With bars high above the sea, right on the beach, and at all altitudes between, you can pickle your liver here more cheaply than in any similar area. It's only a small hyperbole to claim the Caribbean has everything except snow.

The opposite extreme of Caribbean lolling luxury does not get the publicity. Yet it can be the milieu for dreams come true to millions. It is best described by feeling, but feelings are not so easily described as feasts and gaming tables and racing boats. Here is a description of feelings for a little known island by a lady who knows the island well – M. Eugenia Charles, Prime Minister of Dominica:

Dominica – The Nature Island

Of all the islands in our beautiful Caribbean, Dominica stands unique as the one least troubled by the modern age. It is not mere promotion but a simple truth that Dominica is described as 'The Nature Island'.

What this means for persons who may wish to retire here is that they can count on a peace and a serenity that they have probably never encountered anywhere else. It is common for visitors after expressing an intention to 'come again', to declare 'this is the kind of place where I would like to retire'.

A relatively small population for its size, a still developing road and communication network and widely scattered living communities all contribute to the calm and easy-paced life style of Dominica. It is particularly conducive to persons who wish to pass their mature

160

years with the minimum of modern pressures. The lush green mountains and valleys and our hundreds of crystal clear rivers further enhance the soothing atmosphere that everywhere abounds.

A friendly people who do not intrude on your privacy welcome you to Dominica's shores.

The quality of life we presently enjoy is rapidly becoming unavailable anywhere else. We value it. And we invite anyone who may wish to share in the peaceful contentment of Nature's homeland to join us. What is God-given is indeed worth sharing.

Dominica is indeed the place for delightful living.

To feel so deeply about a piece of earth you must have roots that tap deep. When you feel such appreciation for your new homeland you will experience the truth that love given will be love returned. There is space in the Caribbean, space on the not yet spoiled islands to think new thoughts, to believe new beliefs.

The Caribbean is a spiritual United Nations. Each country is piquantly aware of its nationality and its physical differences. Yet through all the countries flows an essence of intangible likenesses. The Caribbean character was born of bravado and quiet suffering, of bloody rebellions erupting from generations of undemanding compliance. They have a stability that both accepts and ignores the flow of conquerors.

The person who drinks deep of this pot pouri on the quiet islands is gradually regenerated with new life themes that are the scions of earlier centuries surviving in modern dress. You will mature as the years pass with the almost immeasurable feeling of achievement when you realise you have moved, not for a new house, not for a second home, not for investment, but for a better way of life.

Post-script

The Promises and the Threats of ten years ago are now in matured evidence.

Of the projected twenty-million-people increase in our time, the expected share has already arrived here. Growth is everywhere. Since there is no growth without change and no change without pain, some islands have felt quite a bit of pain. It is safe to say every island, even the tiny Grenadines, have felt growth.

Some of the growth has fulfilled the promise of more conveniences on medium and small islands. Other growth, the massive financing by non-resident investors, distorts island life, the pace, the culture, the simplicity. If you want to judge which growth came naturally from the existing population and which from exploitation, as the song says, 'All you gotta do is look'.

All over the small islands mom-pop shops are beaming with enlarged inventories and glassed showcases. What you might have known as Ada's Bar will greet you now as Ada's Superette. (Love that 'Superette', Biglittle.)

For the jetters, many a pristine beach is now dominated by a standard blueprint chain hotel trying to look 'West Indian' by means of a hundred potted palms and a conspicuous, unused hammock.

Throughout the Caribbean, convenience is more modernised. The new international telephone network covers all islands except the virtually uninhabited teensiest. Direct dialing to North and South America, Europe; eleven digits and you get *digame* from Madrid. Perhaps the change most difficult to get used to is believing the phones really work. Small plane and ferry services proliferate like inter-urban bus lines. The cost of some items has risen in keeping with the manufacturing country's inflation: things from the USA are up, from Canada not so up. The increase in Oriental goods brings in lower prices.

Those who have been in the Caribbean long enough to have acquired nostalgia, lament the loss of sweet intimacy. Newcomers don't understand. To them it is still all 'adorable'. The difference is that the mainlanders come from areas where the change has been as great but not alleviated by the ubiquitous natural beauty of the islands.

Some of my long-time neighbours periodically threaten to move, because of the noise of a restaurant or the destruction of coral beds by cruise ships, or the deterioration of adolescents imitating TV. So far all of them have returned from house hunting confessing that the mainland is worse. Perhaps not worse in quality but worse in quantity. People are so crowded that there are more things per square mile to be worse. The solution seems to be to stay, to accept and adjust. The difference is relative.

Time has brought a slight change in the emphasis suggested for looking for an island; more investigation of the island's law enforcement. Some governments are a lot more sophisticated than others. Some are already influenced by the 'bad money' of drug traffic. Also if you think to settle below a marina or anchorage, ask whether the boating industry is controlled. Some boats carry holding tanks. If they don't you may find your snorkeling is viewing waving toilet paper instead of seafans. Ask whether the island has noise control. If not, with the increase of restaurants, you may prefer an upwind hillside parcel on a larger island to a more 'darling' location near a beach close to the blast of barbecued amplifiers.

Ten years ago it was smart to buy on a main road with the hope it would be paved. Today you might be better off at the end of an unpaved side strip away from the trucks, the tour buses, the taxis.

Some of the petite islands that would have been too far out for you ten years ago may have become like exurbia now: Nevis, Anguilla, the Grenadines, the 'off-shores' of Puerto Rico — Culebra and Vieques. With good ferry service, 'off-shore' becomes 'protected'.

In general, if the local people complain about government interference, assume this is a plus, at least at first. Islanders are fiercely independent. For centuries they have been almost totally unaccustomed to development restrictions.

The nostalgic moanings from continentals can be viewed with perspective. Nostalgia is a piquant sauce to memory. A few days ago some of us were hanging around the post office. We recalled when the post office was a few inches above the unpaved road. Every time it rained the road flooded. When we got within fifty feet we took off shoes, rolled up pants and waded in. It was fun. Well, while we were talking a squall came. We dashed across the new paved parking lot in our shoes. That wasn't bad, either.

The common-sense, basic rules of moving to the Caribbean have not changed, nor the uncommon tips on locating land and building to take advantage of the climate; the chapters on life-style, gardening, cooking, the dialects are as unchanging as the blue of the sea and the sweetness of the air.

Perhaps the most important change will be in you. Give another thought to old Socrates: 'Know thyself.' Some people get caught in the dilemma of wanting that better Caribbean life but can't give up the fragrance of a quick buck which is wafting among the islands. They want to enter the psychologically richer life yet make money out of it along the way.

You can certainly build and rent in this market.

(*From* Island Properties Report March 1988)

Books on the Caribbean published by Macmillan

Island Guides

Antigua and Barbuda: Heart of the Caribbean
Brian Dyde

Barbados: The Visitor's Guide
Sir Alexander Hoyos

Curacao Close-Up
Bernadette Heiligers-Halabi

Grenada: Isle of Spice
Norma Sinclair

Keeping Company with Jamaica
Sir Philip Sherlock

Montserrat: Emerald Isle of the Caribbean
Howard Fergus

Nevis: Queen of the Caribees
Joyce Gordon

St. Lucia: Helen of the West Indies
Guy Ellis

Masquerade: The Visitor's Introduction to Trinidad and Tobago
Jeremy Taylor

Treasure Islands: A Guide to the British Virgin Islands
Larry and Reba Shepard

Islands to the Windward: Five Gems of the Caribbean
Brian Dyde

Natural Histories

Flowers of the Caribbean
Bill Lennox and Tony Seddon

Trees of the Caribbean
Tony Seddon and Bill Lennox

Fishes of the Caribbean Reefs
Ian Took

Birds of Trinidad and Tobago
Richard ffrench

Butterflies and other Insects of the Eastern Caribbean
Peter Stiling

Marine Life of the Caribbean
A. Jones and N. Sefton

Fruits and Vegetables of the Caribbean
M.J. Bourne, G.W. Lennox and S.A. Seddon

Native Orchids of the Eastern Caribbean
Julian Kenny

History and Historic Background

A Short History of the West Indies — Fourth Edition
J.H. Parry, P.M. Sherlock and A.P. Maingot

Barbados: A History from the Amerindians to Independence
F.A. Hoyos

The Barbados-American Connection
May Lumsden

Historic Buildings of St. Thomas and St. John
W.P. MacLean

The Barbados-Carolina Connection
W. Alleyne and H. Fraser

Island Living

Algae and You: Pool Care in the Sun
Gordon Gutteridge

Ay Ay: An Island Almanac
George Seaman

Cookery

Privilege: Cooking in the Caribbean
Errol Barrow and Kendal Lee

The Cooking of the Caribbean Islands
Linda Wolfe

Recipes: The Cooking of the Caribbean Islands

Cooking the West Indian Way
Dalton Babb